RHYTHMS OF DIALOGUE

PERSONALITY AND PSYCHOPATHOLOGY:

A Series of Monographs, Texts, and Treatises

Rhythms of Dialogue

JOSEPH JAFFE

Department of Communication Sciences
New York State Psychiatric Institute

Department of Psychiatry
College of Physicians and Surgeons
Columbia University

Research Department
The William Alanson White Institute
New York, New York

STANLEY FELDSTEIN

Division of Biological Psychiatry
Department of Psychiatry
New York Medical College

Research Department
The William Alanson White Institute
New York, New York

ACADEMIC PRESS   NEW YORK AND LONDON   1970

ACADEMIC PRESS, INC.
111 Fifth Avenue, New York, New York 10003

United Kingdom Edition published by
ACADEMIC PRESS, INC. (LONDON) LTD.
Berkeley Square House, London W1X 6BA

LIBRARY OF CONGRESS CATALOG CARD NUMBER: 72-107573

PRINTED IN THE UNITED STATES OF AMERICA

This book is dedicated to
our fathers
Benjamin Jaffe
and
Mark Feldstein

v

Contents

Preface

This monograph summarizes a five-year research project on the rhythmic pattern of conversations. It describes an application of the method of interaction chronography to spoken communication. By "rhythm" we refer to the on–off sequence of speech rather than to the stress pattern of words or phrases. Our contribution is threefold. First, we have completely automated the technique of interaction chronography. The complete process, from microphone input to computer-generated statistical summary, is accomplished in a single operation without human intervention. Second, a mathematical model has been developed which constitutes a theory of the way two speech sources interact to generate the conversational rhythm. Finally, we have demonstrated the psychological validity of the model parameters in a series of controlled experiments involving approximately 600 conversations.

Our contribution rests firmly on the pioneering work of many others. The history of interaction chronography can be traced back over thirty years, and the observations essential to a Markovian model of speech rhythms were made twenty years ago. The work reported here weaves these threads together and extends them to dialogue. The project was interdisciplinary and brought together the psychologist, psychiatrist, linguist, engineer, mathematician, statistician, and computer programmer at one time or another. Such projects are perhaps best reported as a series of chapters, each devoted to the work of, and written by one of the specialists. But believing that interdisciplinary fertilization ultimately succeeds only when the disciplines reside in the same skull, we have rather attempted an integrative effort. This, plus the fact that the sequence

of chapters bears close resemblance to the actual history of the
project, may account for some unevenness in the level of complexity.

We are indebted to many people in the conduct of this research,
but primarily to Dr. Louis Cassotta, who designed our automated
system, contributed many of the basic ideas, and whose disserta-
tion constitutes one of the major experiments. It was our good
fortune to obtain the consultation, formal and informal, of Doctors
Jacob Cohen, Alex Heller, Joseph Schwartz, George A. Miller,
Benoit Mandlebrot, Joseph Harrison, David McK. Rioch, Donald
A. Norman, Ascher Opler, and Warren McCullough. The first two
were most actively involved over the years and effectively func-
tioned as co-investigators. We are also indebted to Mrs. Martha
Jane Plimpton for her editorial skill and assistance through the un-
countable retypings of the manuscript, and to Doctors Louis J.
Gerstman and Samuel W. Anderson for their insightful critical
comments thereon.

The research was supported by a grant from the National Institute
of Mental Health and was sponsored by The William Alanson White
Institute in New York City where the majority of the work was conducted. We thank Dr. Lawrence C. Kolb, Chairman, Department of
Psychiatry, Columbia University, whose vision made possible the
completion of the project at The New York State Psychiatric Institute.

A project of this magnitude and duration is basically carried out
by a small army of research assistants too numerous to mention,
but Joanna Chorosh, Helene Goldberg, Carol Toscano, Carol Jean
Rogalski, and Roland Moses are in a different category, and we
gratefully acknowledge their help. It is also traditional for the
authors to thank their wives and children for enduring the day-to-
day turmoil of an enterprise such as this, but its being traditional
does not diminish the sentiment nor deny its truth.

CHAPTER I

INTRODUCTION

A conversation is one of the commonest phenomena we encounter, yet it is one which raises very great scientific problems,
many still unsolved. It is so often our commonest experiences,
which we take for granted, that are most elusive of explanation
and description.

On Human Communication
Colin Cherry, 1961, p. 10

To the best of our knowledge, the method of interaction chronography had two separate origins more than three decades ago. One
version of the technique derived from the field of communication
engineering, and its stated goal was the application of probability
theory to the time sequence of telephonic communication (Norwine
& Murphy, 1938).[1] However, this pioneering effort merely presented probability distributions of events; there was no attempt to
model them or to correlate them with other characteristics of the
speakers. The other source of the technique derives from the field
of social anthropology, and this was its initial application to the
study of personality (Chapple, 1939). Here the aim was the quantification of time sequences of gross behavior, including but not
limited to speech, in face-to-face interaction.[2] Neither of these early

---

[1] We actually achieve this early goal in Chapters IV and V which deal with probabilistic modeling of time sequences of dialogue. A development parallel to our
own, and a more direct descendant of the pioneering study, is attributable to Brady
(1968, 1969).

[2] The history of interaction chronography is considered in greater detail in Chapter
II.

applications had a *primarily* linguistic focus; nor for that matter does our own, which essentially combines the two approaches with the addition of certain paralinguistic considerations.

Our initial interest was the study of dyadic interaction in the framework of psychotherapy research. This application dictated a focus upon certain interpersonal or *system* features of conversation that might be relevant to the communication of mood, to the phenomenon of "empathy" and to the breakdown of effective dialogue. Investigations of such problems are confronted with a mass of clinical interview material which, in all its richness, is largely unmanageable. Expediency, therefore, led us to concentrate on the on–off patterns of vocal signals in face-to-face conversation. This restriction simplified the transduction of signals via the use of voice-actuated relays, and made large scale automated data processing possible. We realized, however, that the meaningful pursuit of our initial interest called for a comparable body of knowledge about the temporal structure of nonclinical conversations. The task proved more demanding of time and more intriguing than we had expected, and our efforts to fulfill the task form the substance of this monograph.

Some of the technological solutions adopted posed the problem of relating our findings to those of other disciplines. For example, the most sophisticated studies of speech rhythms employ the sound spectrograph (Liberman, Cooper, Shankweiler, & Studdert-Kennedy, 1967) and even the electromyograph (Cooper, 1966). The former demonstrates brief interruptions in the energy pattern of the speech signal which are referable to phenomena such as stop consonants. Such pauses are not perceived by the naive listener and are purposely bridged by our speech detector, which also confounds juncture pauses with hesitation pauses and linguistic with nonlinguistic vocalizations. Thus, it is at present difficult to relate the two domains of measurement in a manner that would be satisfactory to investigators of acoustic phonetics. It is nevertheless possible to point to certain correspondences between our indices and the more properly linguistic ones of phonemic clause, terminal juncture, and syntactic boundaries (see Chapters II and III).

The serious study of dialogue patterns makes one poignantly aware that the largest unit dealt with in contemporary linguistics is at most the monologue and, more typically, the isolated sentence. Thus, there is a dearth of theory regarding the grosser dialogic phenomena which are of primary interest here. For example, little is known about the linguistic determinants of a switch from the listening to speaker roles (or the reverse), or about the mutual influence of the rhythmic patterns of speakers. This hiatus in the available background information was responsible for the progressive shift in our research emphasis from the interview format to the study of spontaneous, unstructured, "natural" dialogue. Hence, this monograph maps and explores the gross temporal structure of an area that will eventually have to be dealt with by linguistic science.

It seems appropriate to summarize here certain major findings of the research. They are introduced at this point as a general guide to the reader and as a frame of reference which integrates the specialized concerns of the subsequent chapters. They also suggest the outlines of a tentative theory of the temporal structure of dialogue to be amplified in Chapter VI.

(1) A completely automated system can encode the on–off characteristics of conversation more reliably than a human observer and in a form suitable for deeper mathematical analysis.

(2) The temporal patterns of conversation have a formal structure, unambiguously definable by an automated system as a sequence of units in time. This structure shows certain mathematical properties which are relatively invariant in the conversations we have examined.

(3) The mean values of some of these units are stable characteristics of speakers; others are less stable and consequently serve as sensitive indices of the interaction.

(4) The mean values can be systematically modified as a function of social context.

(5) A key feature of the dialogic rhythm is the fact that one speaker at a time holds the floor with concomitant suppression of simultaneous speech. We presume this phenonenon to be a linguistic universal, to a great extent neurophysiologically obligatory, and based on the information processing limitations of the nervous system. Simultaneous speaking and listening is extremely difficult without dysfluency and/or loss of comprehension.

(6) There is a strong tendency for speakers in conversation to match the average durations of the pauses that they alternately exhibit while speaking. This is not generally true of the durations of their respective vocalizations (as we measure them). This pause matching phenomenon is probably responsible for the positive correlations which several investigators have obtained between the average lengths of time that interacting speakers "hold the floor" (Matarazzo, Wiens, Saslow, Allen, & Weitman, 1964). The mutual pacing is referable to a bilateral adjustment of silence intervals, and this may correlate with phenomena such as empathy or communication of mood. It is a conceivable mechanism for adjusting the linguistic information processing rates of the speakers to each other.

(7) We have succeeded in modeling the simple sound – silence sequence of both monologue and dialogue as stochastic processes, and have demonstrated the utility of a rule, first proposed by Jaffe and Norman (1964), which specifies the interdependence of the participants in a dialogue. The implications for monologue, viewed as a two-state Markov chain with but a 300 millisecond constraint between transitions, are that over the range that the model fits (98% of the pause and vocalization events) the durations of adjacent pauses and vocalizations must be statistically independent. Furthermore, continuing to pause or speak should be independent of how long one has been doing so. This raises questions regarding recent observations of long range constraints in the on–off patterns of monologue (Goldman-Eisler, 1968), and suggests that the phenomena are attributable to random fluctuations rather than underlying cognitive states of the speaker (Schwartz & Jaffe, 1968).

Analogous modeling of the temporal sequence of dialogue with the same short range constraint implies that the duration of holding the floor between utterances of the other speaker cannot be related to the length of time the preceding speaker held the floor within a single dialogue. This conclusion too is surprising in view of recent research (Ray and Webb, 1966) on the "question–answer effect," i.e., on the average, the longer the question, the longer the answer. The implications we draw are, of course, limited by the degree to which the model fits and to our methods of measuring these durations, but they do suggest that certain lines of research may be unfruitful.

The seven points summarize the major findings reported in Chapters II through VI. They lead to certain tentative theoretical formulations which are implicit in our working assumptions and theoretical predilections. The most important of these assumptions is that dialogue is the unit of verbal interaction, and that monologue is a special case of dialogue in which one participant is silent or absent. This assumption derives from considerations of language development and from our interpersonal or systems approach. It receives anecdotal support in the following statement by Roman Jakobson (1964, pp. 162–163).

> Not only for verbal pathology but for the field of communication in general, it is important to realize that the monologue is a very complex superstructure, unfamiliar to many ethnic and social groups. Some field-workers, anxious not to interfere with the native informant and to learn his unconstrained, natural speech, would ask the native to tell the story of his life. This is, however, the grossest constraint which can be imagined, because . . . to tell a story outside the frame of a dialogue, and without being interrupted, is for many natives an utterly artificial situation. A brilliant Russian linguist, L. Shcherba (1915. Vostochno-luzhickoe narechie, Petrograd) made observations among Lusatian Sorbs and found that in their communities the monologue simply doesn't exist. Only one form of monologue does occur in such societies, and this is the cliché monologue, the ready-made ritual performance—a prayer or a ceremonial speech.

No human has ever learned to speak except in a dialogic context, so to this extent the ability to speak presupposes a prior conversation. It is also relevant to our assumption that while monologic time patterns can be extracted from dialogue, it is not obvious at present how a dialogic rhythm can be constructed from two pure monologues. We do not assert that the latter is impossible, but simply that the necessary interaction parameters are not apparent in pure monologue.

At a more speculative level, there is a theoretical issue which is relevant to an ultimate application of the methodology we present to studies of communication pathology, and which, therefore, deserves at least a provisional statement.

It would not be surprising to discover a strong biological component underlying social forms, e.g., in the politeness prescriptions for conversational good manners. The ideal physical requirements for speech production, transmission, and reception (without the use of electronic devices) require that breathing be regulated, the mouth be unencumbered by objects that interfere with articulation, volume of voice be adjusted to speaking distance, the ears be generally uncovered, speakers face each other, etc. Thus are there admonitions such as "Catch your breath before starting to talk," "Take your fingers out of your mouth," "Swallow your food before speaking," "Don't shout," "Look at me when I address you," "Speak up." The phenomena described in points (5) and (6) above suggest further interactional rules that govern the matching of speech rates of the participants, the prohibition of interruption, and the requirement for properly timed signals that acknowledge understanding and confirm the continued attention of the listener. These too may have intelligible biological foundations to which our results can point. However, rules such as "Don't speak unless spoken to," although related to biosocial phenomena such as pecking order, demonstrate wider variations, which are the proper concern of sociolinguistics and social anthropology.

In short, we are suggesting that: (a) it is possible, and may be profitable, to entertain the notion of a set of "rules" which underlie what might be termed "interactional skill"; and (b) at least several of such "rules" are the necessary consequences of the finite information processing capacities of the neural apparatus. The rhythmic elements of this skill may be independent of the semantic aspects of meaningful discourse as suggested by Sullivan's (1947, p. 165) assertion that

> On the wards of larger mental hospitals, one sometimes can listen in, as it were, to a "conversation" between two of the dilapidated patients who have come to find each other's company inoffensive. The remarks of each are made with due regard for the principle that only one person should be speaking at a time. There may be considerable intonational coloring, as if, for example, questions were being asked and answered, or as if one had reminded the other of something astonishing to him. The remarks, however, have but the most remote, if any, connection with those of the other. Each is talking to himself, but is doing it in a sort of double solitaire played after the fashion of conventional language behavior.[3]

These rules of dialogue are unformalized at present, yet their relevance to research in disordered communication should not be missed. Their proper assessment would require a body of normative

---

[3] From *Conceptions of Modern Psychiatry* by Harry Stack Sullivan, by permission of W. W. Norton & Company, Inc., copyright 1940, 1945, 1947, 1953 by The William Alanson White Psychiatric Foundation.

data which do not yet exist, and to which the present research is but a beginning contribution.

Finally, certain specialized aspects and interdependencies of the subsequent chapters deserve comment as a guide to the reader. In Chapter II, the phenomena of conversational rhythms which are of primary interest are first discussed, followed by a brief review of the history of interaction chronography as it applies to the problem of encoding vocal time patterns. Our instrumentation is then described, along with the considerations that led to the classification scheme we finally employed. The effects of the instrumentation upon the true events which it claims to represent are considered, and we make clear where our observations overlap the distinctions of interest to linguists and where they do not. The exponential distributions of the classified events are presented, and suggestions offered for extensions of the methodology to areas of research beyond the scope of this monograph.

Chapter III presents the substance of our experimental data, roughly in terms of the major issues with which we were concerned. At the same time, the sequence in which the experiments were conducted is made explicit in order to provide the reader with a sense of the emergence of new questions from the results of one experiment which structured the design of the next. The rationale for this plan of presentation is discussed in the Preface. Full comprehension of this chapter presumes some understanding of inferential statistics. Short of this, the essential findings should be clear to the less sophisticated reader. The chapter concludes with a report of a pilot study, somewhat peripheral to the main thrust of the work, but included to point out again the possible articulation of our approach with the primary concerns of linguistics.

Chapter IV is an exercise in stochastic modeling and assumes familiarity with elementary probability theory. A rather tutorial introduction to the restructuring of our data as a Markov process is included on the advice of behavioral scientists in several fields. The notion was that the monograph might then be more useful in mathematical models seminars. The initiated may skip this introductory section and proceed to the presentation of the Markov models. The chapter concludes with a reanalysis of one of the experiments of the previous chapter to assess the predictive capability of the best of the models. The "goodness of fit" score employed, the Neyman-Pearson statistic, is justified as the appropriate means for comparing stochastic processes, but may be treated simply as a score by the reader unconcerned with such matters.

Chapter V effects a synthesis of the two major approaches presented in the monograph up to that point. Drawing upon the major experimental findings of Chapter III, which in turn employed the descriptive classification of Chapter II, a new stochastic process is proposed. Its unique feature is the use of the psychological hypothesis underlying the descriptive classification for the automatic computer classification of inferred behavioral states. The psychological hypothesis is that one speaker in dialogue always holds the floor as decided by a "speaker switching rule." The rule is realized as an automaton which transduces or maps the sequence of observed behavioral states into another hypothetical sequence of states. The latter is then analyzed as a Markov chain. This final model explains why the models presented in Chapter IV, in which states are defined in a way that violates intuition, account for the data as well as they did. The previous models are seen to be special cases of the one now proposed, and for a reason which is of considerable psychological interest, namely, our empirical finding that interacting speakers match their pause distributions. Furthermore, the final model is completely equivalent to the descriptive classification when applied to the time pattern of unstructured dialogue. This synthesis is presented as a demonstration only, inasmuch as a reanalysis of all the experiments reported is not feasible at present, would be unlikely to alter the major findings, and would unduly delay the appearance of the monograph. This chapter requires a thorough assimilation of the preceding ones. It also includes a simplified explanation of lumpable Markov chains.

Chapters II through V lack individual summaries. Because of the varied complexity of the chapters, we decided to incorporate the summaries in the concluding Chapter VI in order to provide, hopefully, a facilitative overview.

The Appendixes present the design of our electronic instrumentation, a reliability study performed thereon, and certain statistical details that may be of specialized interest.

CHAPTER II

A DESCRIPTIVE CLASSIFICATION OF
CONVERSATIONAL RHYTHMS

In this chapter we propose a logically coherent descriptive classification of the temporal characteristics of dialogue. The taxonomy
is intuitively reasonable, having been arrived at by other investigators as well, and corresponds to the commonsense perception of
events. Using this classification scheme, measures appropriate to
the study of the temporal patterning of conversation are identified.
An automated system for quantification of these time parameters is
also described.

I. The Speaker Switch

Perhaps the most salient feature of ordinary face-to-face conversation is its oscillating rhythm. We say that speakers alternately
have the floor, i.e., vocal activity switches periodically from one
speaker to the other. It follows that they speak simultaneously only
a small percentage of the time. This feature of dialogue has been
nominated by Miller (1963, p. 418) for the status of a "language
universal."

One wonders, of course, how complete this catalogue of universals really
is. There is such variety and richness among the language universals listed
here — each painstakingly documented by studies in many different languages
— that one hesitates to suggest that anything might be missing. But consider,
for example, the remarkable fact that conversational partners alternate between talking and listening. This reciprocity, which I assume is universal,

is not a necessary consequence of any auditory or physiological inability to speak and hear simultaneously; one voice is poor masking noise for another. There is no *a priori* reason why two people who have questions to ask one another could not question simultaneously and answer simultaneously. Nevertheless, we alternate. There are several interesting lines of speculation one might pursue from such a language universal — if it is indeed universal. Perhaps there is some limit imposed by agility and attention, perhaps some critical component of the speech apparatus must be actively involved in the process of understanding speech, etc.

The "speaker switching" phenomenon is the first concept discussed because it is the keystone of our classification scheme. It is the interface between the respective monologues into which conversation may be decomposed. In most dialogues, a switch occurs after a brief intervening period of mutual silence. A direct transition (i.e., without perceptible pause) from the vocalization of one speaker to that of the other occurs in only about 25% of the exchanges as we measure them. This suggests that an interval of silence is required to transform a listener into a speaker. During the utterance of either speaker, which can include momentary pauses with resumption of talking, that of the other seems almost completely suppressed. We may think of this temporal reciprocity as establishing a kind of "territoriality phenomenon" in the time domain; the available time is partitioned between the speakers, and they tend to agree about possession of the floor. The boundaries of these partitions are blurred, however, since the bridge of silence at the switching point is in some sense joint property.[1]

The intuitive appeal of the unit so demarcated, i.e., the individual time domains between switches, has led a prominent linguist to define an *utterance unit* as "all the speech of one participant until the other participant begins to speak" (Fries, 1952). We shall build upon this definition.

The phenomenon seems unremarkable at first. It may be dismissed (although not explained) as ordinary "politeness," as a socially learned rule of verbal interaction. The general adherence to this rule permits the application of appealingly simple stimulus–

---

[1]To pursue the territoriality analogy even a step further, a speaker may occasionally intrude, i.e., vocalize during the other's vocalization or momentary pause. Thus, the territories themselves are not totally inviolate.

response models to conversation. The active speaker is considered the message source, and the inactive speaker the destination. We immediately recognize the classic model of communication theory, the "one-way channel." In the interval between switches, a model of a one-way channel is adequate since the transmitter and receiver roles appear to remain fixed. An explanation for the switch of roles is still required, however. We look to the cues operative at the boundary between time domains. The utterance of each speaker is presumably terminated by an unambiguous "end of message" signal, at which point the direction of the one-way channel (and the transmitting and receiving roles) are simply reversed. It is tempting as an initial approximation to consider each utterance as the response to that of the previous speaker and, at the same time, as a stimulus to his subsequent utterance. The intervening silence between the end of one speaker's message and the beginning of the other's might then be envisaged as a reaction time.[2] This idealized model is realized in telegraphic or radio communication when the end of message signal ("Over") is followed by the intentional closing of a switch in order to put the complete one-way channel at the disposal of the other participant. As an artifact of instrumentation, the idealized model is also artificially realized in telephonic "lockout" circuits and in certain voice-actuated interaction chronographs. In these circuits, the speech of one of two participants pre-empts the channel while in progress and for some fixed length of time following its cessation, thereby making interruption physically impossible and/or unrecordable. Where a one-way rule exists, either by social convention or artifactually by instrumentation, vocal activity of the dialogue participants is totally asynchronous. It alternates neatly and politely without overlap of the time domains of the two speakers. Asynchrony is thus the rule and synchrony (simultaneous speech) the violation in conversational vocal patterns. Choral speaking, singing, and cheering are exceptions

---

[2] This initial approximation derives from stimulus–response psychology and disregards the "planning" and anticipatory activities of the listener as he decodes and prepares to respond (Miller, Galanter, & Pribram, 1964). We shall show in Chapter III that the reaction time assumption is unsatisfactory in natural dialogues, although perhaps warranted in highly structured "question-answer" interviews.

which prove the rule. The vocalizers in these activities operate as a single source, in which case asynchrony is as disruptive as is synchrony in two-source dialogue. One need but imagine the choir member who starts singing a beat before the others or ends a beat late.

II. Overview of Interaction Chronography

The rhythm of dialogue is usually investigated by means of an interaction chronograph or one of its descendants. The earliest application of which we are aware provides a comprehensive classification (Norwine & Murphy, 1938, p. 282), difficult to improve upon today. It is quoted here in its entirety simply because its major features will be found under a slightly different nomenclature in our own descriptive classification.

> A *talkspurt* is speech by one party, including his pauses, which is preceded and followed, with or without intervening pauses, by speech from the other party perceptible to the one producing the talkspurt. Obvious exceptions to this definition are the initial and final talkspurts in a conversation. There may be simultaneous talkspurts by the two talkers; if one party is speaking and at the same time hears speech from the other *double talking* is said to occur.
>
> *Resumption time* is the length of the pause intervening between two periods of speech within a talkspurt.
>
> *Response time* is the length of the interval between the beginning of a pause as heard by the listener and the beginning of his reply. It may be positive or negative. The pause to which reference is made ordinarily occurs at the end of a talkspurt but may be a pause followed by a resumption of speech by the first talker.[3]

The goal of this codification was the application of probability theory to the temporal patterning of telephonic communication. "The specific information desired was the probability that a conversational element would have any given duration t" (Norwine & Murphy, 1938, p. 283).

The technique of interaction chronography was first employed

---

[3] Note that the silence between vocalization of two different speakers is conceptualized as a reaction time for the second, which we shall show to be questionable. The remainder of this definition is logically somewhat confused, since a negative response time is an inference regarding double talking.

for the study of personality by Chapple (1939), and this application is consequently more familiar to behavioral scientists. Since tracking was done by a human observer, a higher degree of motivational inference could be used, and the category names reflect this, e.g., interruptions, initiative, and dominance.

All subsequent developments may be seen as refinements of these original techniques and observations. Whereas the vocal signal was written automatically by a recording oscillograph in the Norwine and Murphy study, the measurements were made manually from a paper strip recording. The Chapple instrument required a human observer to follow the interaction by depressing one or both of two keys, each corresponding to one of the participants. The key was operated when the respective participant was "acting," the action being either vocalization, gesture, or a combination of the two. The remaining computation of the occurrence of the interactive events and cumulative counts thereof was automated. Subsequent efforts of various behavioral scientists have been in the direction of automating the total sequence, i.e., dispensing with the human observer at both the observation end and the measurement end. This effectively amounts to a wedding of the Norwine and Murphy system to the Chapple system. Perhaps for this reason, the trend has been toward progressive emphasis upon the vocalized portion of the message system to the neglect of the gestural, since this aspect is most amenable to automatic recording by means of a voice key. How much of the conversational rhythm is being neglected by this expedient solution? It has been stated that in face-to-face interviews, a very high percentage of acts are congruent with vocal "utterances." Recent studies (Dittman & Llewellyn, 1969, p. 98) show matters to be somewhat more complex: "The data collected by this method allowed direct test of statements by Pittenger *et al.* (1960), and by Scheflen (1964), whose claims of very close speech–movement relationships were found to be exaggerated."

A review of the literature on the rhythmic patterns of verbal interaction indicates that criteria vary greatly from one study to another. This is somewhat surprising since the decision as to when a speaker starts, pauses, or stops would seem to be a straightforward task. Nevertheless, it is difficult to find reports which use comparable criteria even in the case of extended periods of monologue. For dialogues, and for multilogues, the situation is even more chaotic. A conceptual confusion between individual criteria and interpersonal or transactional criteria appears to occur in descriptions of the verbal interaction of two or more speakers. This will be further clarified later in this chapter. For the moment, we note and illustrate at least four types of compromise with a completely non-inferential behavioral classification of temporal patterns of vocalization in dialogue. They are often intentional, although sometimes forced by practical necessity.

(1) Arbitrary cut-off points may be established based on the investigator's interest in units of certain durations, i.e., categories may be defined in light of some prior guess as to their significance.

For example, investigators of verbal interaction have generally shown a preference either for study of sound burst distributions or of pause distributions but, curiously, rarely for both. The Hargreaves-Starkweather Duration Tabulator (Hargreaves & Starkweather, 1959) yielded silence rather than a speech distribution by reversal of the signal. Investigators concerned solely with the unitizing of the sound burst signal may arbitrarily define a pause for that purpose alone. For instance, Meltzer, Hayes, and Shellenberger (1966) studied sound durations as a measure of dyadic interaction. However, the distribution of pauses, their durations and their perceptual consequences have been extensively studied in their own right. Goldman-Eisler (1958) categorizes those of less than 0.25 second as "articulatory pauses" and those of greater length as "hesitation pauses."

(2) Purely temporal criteria may be confounded with inferential criteria, e.g., judgments derived from the pragmatic, syntactic, or semantic levels of language.

For example, the early work of Hargreaves (1960) employed *both* a transactional and an individual definition of utterance. The unit was terminated by the listener's response and also when "there was no evidence of intent to continue within the next second or two." In later work, such inferential criteria were dropped, and the unit simply terminated when a speaker paused for some arbitrary duration.

(3) Temporal patterns of vocalization may be confounded with

those of gestural activity. The latter may be concurrent with, or independent of, the vocal activity.

For example, in the extensive body of research using Chapple's Interaction Chronograph, the vocal and gestural cues were intentionally confounded in the observer instruction which stated that "all facial (and other) muscle activity must have come to an end for action to be scored as ceased." Gesture, therefore, was also scored as action. In principle, the Chapple instrument could be applied to a conversation in a completely nonvocal communication system, e.g., in the manual language of the deaf. It is fair to say that the purpose of this instrument originally was the study of "action" units rather than speech per se. However, these units of action were subsequently used as the basis for "utterance length" and "silence" scores, and it is difficult to relate them unequivocally to unconfounded speech studies.[4]

(4) In the case of human observers, certain complex interaction patterns may simply exceed the discriminative capacities of the operator. For example, using Chapple's Interaction Chronograph, it was found that lowest observer reliability occurred in those sections of the interview in which both participants were speaking at the same time (Saslow & Matarazzo, 1959). In our own work comparing automated with manual interaction chronography, we have also found that a human observer was able to achieve high reliability in the absence of simultaneous speech. However, this reliability dropped sharply when the more complicated type of discrimination was required (Appendix B).

Apart from these conceptual and/or observational inconsistencies among studies, the sheer impact on the data of varying instrumentation and sampling procedures is formidable. Various recording systems have been described by Kasl and Mahl (1956), Verzeano and Finesinger (1949), Shapiro (1964), and others, in addition to those previously cited. The goals varied in all these studies from linguistic analysis to gross encoding of overall activity levels or sequences. Some used analog to digital conversion of vocal signals, whereas others summarized the distribution of durations of events

---

[4]A method for obtaining unconfounded measures of vocal interaction has recently been described by Wiens, Molde, Holman, and Matarazzo (1966) who use the Chapple instrument.

by logic circuits which increment counters for successively longer time intervals.

Perhaps the most detailed methodology as far as the pure temporal analysis of vocal interaction is concerned is that of Brady (1968, 1969). His approach is closest to our own in that it utilizes analog to digital conversion and computer analysis thereof in a completely automated system. Yet even here there is a lack of correspondence of descriptive classification, sampling rates, and methods of handling minimal durations of sound and silence. A comparison of our instrument and Brady's and their effects on data are given in Appendix A. At this point, however, his work is cited as an exemplary analysis of dialogic rhythm from the communication engineering point of view. Were the previously cited contributions to interaction chronography documented with similar precision, a genuine comparative analysis of this area of research might be feasible.

This brief overview illustrates some of the difficulties encountered in comparing the findings of different investigators. We conclude that such comparison would be facilitated by a logically consistent set of definitions. However, there are two barriers to such codification. The first is technological; the degree and precision of quantification is a function of the instrumentation currently available to the investigator. The second and perhaps more interesting limitation is conceptual; an extremely clear distinction is required between the use of gestural and vocal cues. A firm decision must be made as to whether to consider syntax, inferred motivation, etc., in addition to the simple presence or absence of a vocal signal as the basis for the temporal pattern. Obviously, a voice relay will only be sensitive to the latter. Thus, if a pause is to be considered nonexistent because it occurs within some continuous linguistic unit (such as a word or phrase), then information is being taken into account over and above the pure pattern of energy distribution as recorded by a voice relay. Another important conceptual determinant is the question of whether the unitizing criteria are individual, transactional (dyadic), or both. It is clear that although there is a general consensus developing in this investigative area, the notation system is in a somewhat unresolved state. An approach to the clarification of these issues is now presented.

III. Encoding of Time Patterns

We first describe a completely automated system for the analysis of conversational rhythms. The system automatically encodes the sequences of sounds and silences from live or tape recorded discourse and is shown in Figure II-1. The analog voltage signal of each speaker's channel triggers a voice relay which is periodically sampled for presence or absence of speech. The sampling rate throughout the studies reported in this monograph was 200 per minute. Vocalization during the sampling period is recorded on

FIGURE II-1. The Automatic Vocal Transaction Analyzer (AVTA) system. On the far right is an Ampex two-channel tape recorder, remotely connected to a recording studio (not shown). To its left, in the following order, are: the AVTA unit proper, the PDP 8/I computer, and the teletype. The latter produces both a punched paper tape of the analog to digital conversion (for input to other programs) and printed summary statistics. (Photograph courtesy of The New York State Psychiatric Institute.)

punched paper tape and is also sensed by an on-line digital computer. The format of the punched tape output is illustrated in Figure II-2.[5]

In this analog to digital conversion, sound is defined by the presence of a punch and silence by its absence. Successive punches are defined as continuous vocalization, successive spaces as continuous silence. The sequence of holes and spaces depicts the sound–silence patterns of an individual speaker or a dyadic interaction.

A human judgment enters, of course, into the time constant and threshold settings of the voice relays, and this constitutes an important theoretical decision which partially defines the phenomena we choose to encode. Each dialogue is initially monitored by an operator who observes the opening and closing of the relays as displayed visually. The instrument is then set so that the relay operation corresponds to the natural commonsense perception of sound burst and pause in speech. It is this pattern to which our instrument "listens." There is no attempt to discriminate units that are of interest to descriptive linguists, such as phonemes, morphemes, and stress patterns. Such units are separated only if their pattern of energy distribution is such as to introduce obvious intervals of silence discernible by the naive, untrained ear. The reason for this decision was our concern with certain psychological aspects of the communication process which dictated that we encode speech as heard *by the dialogue participants* rather than by the specially trained linguist. Thus, we have proceeded according to a criterion of naive perception of temporal patterns while remaining aware that other criteria might be used (Appendix A).

A descriptive classification of dialogic rhythm is now presented which will be utilized throughout the monograph. Note that all definitions are transactional, i.e., the definition of each category depends upon the behavior of *both* speakers.

IV. Descriptive Classification

The classification scheme is based on two empirically defined concepts.

---

[5] The sampling characteristics of the system are described in Appendix A.

A. DEFINITION 1: "A CONVERSATION"

For our present purpose, a conversation is a sequence of sounds and silences generated by two (or more) interacting speakers. The sounds and silences may be unilateral, i.e., a single speaker talks, or remains silent when another talks, or they may be bilateral (or multilateral), i.e., joint speaking or joint silence.

B. DEFINITION 2: "POSSESSION OF THE FLOOR"

The speaker who utters the first unilateral sound both initiates the conversation and gains possession of the floor. Having gained possession, a speaker maintains it until the first unilateral sound by another speaker, at which time the latter gains possession of the floor. The conversation terminates at its last sound.

Definition 1 states that there must be at least two speakers in a conversation. Definition 2 implies that a conversation cannot begin with joint sound or joint silence, since such a bilateral (symmetrical) configuration would not assign the floor to either speaker. Another implication is that one and only one speaker holds the floor at every instant of a conversation. Still another is that a conversation cannot end in joint silence.

These two definitions, i.e., of a "conversation" and of "possession of the floor," permit a computer program to classify a dialogue unambiguously into the following five categories.

(1) A *speaker switch* occurs whenever a speaker loses possession of the floor. The times between switches are "floor times," and are synonymous with the definition of utterance in Chapters IV and V.

(2) A *vocalization* is a continuous sound by the speaker who has the floor.

(3) A *pause* is a period of joint silence bounded by the vocalizations of the speaker who has the floor.

(4) A *switching pause* is a period of joint silence bounded by the vocalizations of different speakers, i.e., terminated by a speaker switch. Since it is within the floor time of the speaker who loses the floor, it is assigned to that speaker.

(5) *Simultaneous speech* is a sound by the speaker who does not have the floor during a vocalization by the speaker who does.

These five categories are defined symmetrically for the two

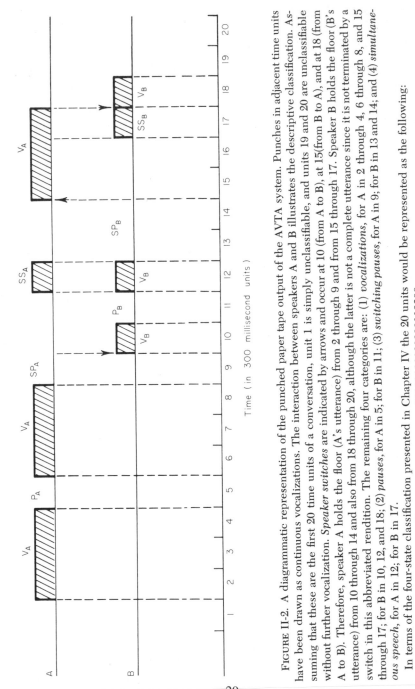

FIGURE II-2. A diagrammatic representation of the punched paper tape output of the AVTA system. Punches in adjacent time units have been drawn as continuous vocalizations. The interaction between speakers A and B illustrates the descriptive classification. Assuming that these are the first 20 time units of a conversation, unit 1 is simply unclassifiable, and units 19 and 20 are unclassifiable without further vocalization. *Speaker switches* are indicated by arrows and occur at 10 (from A to B), at 15(from B to A), and at 18 (from A to B). Therefore, speaker A holds the floor (A's utterance) from 2 through 9 and from 15 through 17. Speaker B holds the floor (B's utterance) from 10 through 14 and also from 18 through 20, although the latter is not a complete utterance since it is not terminated by a switch in this abbreviated rendition. The remaining four categories are: (1) *vocalizations*, for A in 2 through 4, 6 through 8, and 15 through 17; for B in 10, 12, and 18; (2) *pauses*, for A in 5; for B in 11; (3) *switching pauses*, for A in 9; for B in 13 and 14; and (4) *simultaneous speech*, for A in 12; for B in 17.

In terms of the four-state classification presented in Chapter IV the 20 units would be represented as the following:

$$0111011102030011320.$$

In terms of the six-state classification presented in Chapter V the first unit is unclassifiable, and the remainder is represented as the following sequence: A1, A1, A1, A0, A1, A1, A0, B2, B0, B2, B3, B0, B0, A1, A1, A3, B2, B0, B0.

speakers, yielding ten potential parameters of the conversational time sequence. Note, however, that there cannot be a difference of more than one between the speaker switching frequencies of the two participants. It is, therefore, treated as a single dyadic parameter in the experiments of Chapters III and IV. The remaining categories lend themselves to quantification in terms of their mean values. In practice, however, we have treated simultaneous speech as a single dyadic parameter as well. The decision to do so may have been an unfortunate one, but at the time it was made, we were not interested in simultaneous speech. It could, of course, be attributable completely to one speaker if it always occurred when he did not have possession of the floor.

One might also ask whether there ought not to be a category for listening pauses. Such a category would simply be the complement of the active speaker's floor time and would not contribute any new information to a characterization of dialogue. Figure II-2 is a graphic representation of the sound–silence sequence of a portion of conversation which illustrates the descriptive classification.

A peripheral point at the moment, but one which becomes important in Chapters IV and V, may be noted in passing. Note what would happen as the sequence is scanned *from left to right* if we did not remember *at each instant* which speaker had possession of the floor, i.e., if we did not recall the direction of the last speaker switch. Unilateral vocalization by either speaker would recall the information; however, a prolonged run of bilateral behavior (joint silence or simultaneous speech) would be impossible to assign to either speaker. Simultaneous speech is short lived. Since joint silence can, however, be indefinitely prolonged, we would be forced to confound the four silence categories, namely, the pauses and switching pauses of both speakers. This would give us but a single (dyadic) silence state and a single (dyadic) simultaneous speech state, which becomes a crucial issue in our later investigation of stochastic models of these sequences.

V. Linguistic Information in the Descriptive Classification

It is clear that a voice relay cannot make linguistic discriminations of syntax, stress, juncture, pitch, etc. Reduced to the measurement of sheer duration of sound energy above or below a fixed threshold, and disregarding the potential distortions introduced by analog to digital conversion,[6] how do the categories of the descriptive classification relate to the information deemed important by the descriptive linguist?

Simultaneous speech can be dispensed with first, since it is virtually unacknowledged in the concerns of contemporary linguistics, as indeed is the very structure of dialogue. Our average duration of simultaneous speech is roughly .4 second, the only important point being that it is of much shorter duration than the average vocalization. This suggests that an inhibitory process in one or both speakers is operative to terminate this event.

Turning to uninterrupted vocalizations, the mean duration which we observe in natural dialogue $\approx$ 1.64 seconds. Subjectively, this feels like the duration of some syntactic unit, and a reasonable conjecture is the phonemic clause (Trager & Smith, 1951). This rhythmical unit in talking is a string of 2–10 words, averaging 5, in which there is one and only one primary stress and which is terminated by a juncture, a slight slowing of speech, often with slight intonation changes at the very end. A growing body of research has mounted a convincing argument that this unit is important in both encoding and decoding of speech (Boomer, 1965; Dittman & Llewellyn, 1967). What is the average duration of a phonemic clause? This is a difficult measurement, since juncture pauses (which have linguistic significance) are facultative and may be absent between clauses, whereas the modal hesitation pause (a paralinguistic phenonemon) occurs after the first word of a phonemic clause. A voice relay confounds these two types of pauses, but the errors tend to offset each other as far as clause units are concerned. That is, an absent juncture pause splices two clauses together, making our measured vocalization longer than a phonemic clause; a hesitation pause splits the clause, making the measured vocalization shorter than clause length.

Dittman[7] has been kind enough to provide his measurements of phonemic clause length, based on a sampling of 10 fluent and 10 nonfluent clauses from social conversations of each of 3 male and 3 female students. He finds a mean duration of 1.53 seconds which, surprisingly, is similar to our mean vocalization duration! So in

---

[6]These are discussed in Appendix A.

[7]Allan T. Dittman, personal communication, 1968.

spite of the confounding of various types of pause and the splicing of consecutive clauses, the net effect is that the voice relay is roughly estimating mean phonemic clause durations.

It has been impossible to discuss the vocalization durations without invoking the pauses which segment them. The voice relay confounds hesitation and juncture pauses; yet the descriptive classification distinguishes switching pauses from those following which the same speaker holds the floor. The latter are composed both of hesitation pauses and of those juncture pauses which do not result in a switch. There is, however, good evidence from our work, and that of other investigators, that switching pauses are largely juncture pauses. Our evidence is presented in a pilot study at the end of Chapter III. Studies of "listener responses," i.e., speaker switches, also confirm the special nature of switching pauses, since it was shown that nine-tenths of such responses (in telephone-like conversations) did indeed occur following junctures (Dittman & Llewellyn, 1967).

Boomer (1965) reports a value of .75 second for hesitation pauses and 1.03 seconds for juncture pauses. Our studies of unstructured dialogue show average values of about .66 second for pauses and .77 second for switching pauses. While the difference between the last two values is not significant, it will be useful to retain the distinction in order to differentiate highly structured from unstructured conversations in Chapter III. The stochastic models of Chapters IV and V do not make the distinction, and in those chapters the differences between pauses and switching pauses are attributed to a presumably negligible decision time as the listener opts to speak.

VI. Effect of the Apparatus on the Classification

The precision with which the starting and stopping of concurrent vocalizations is determined varies with the sensitivity of the instrument setting. A finer grained sampling would resolve many apparently synchronous starts and stops and, as a result, convert such samples from one category to another.

The transactional definition of the parameters and their sensitivity to settings of the apparatus can be illustrated from Figure II-2.

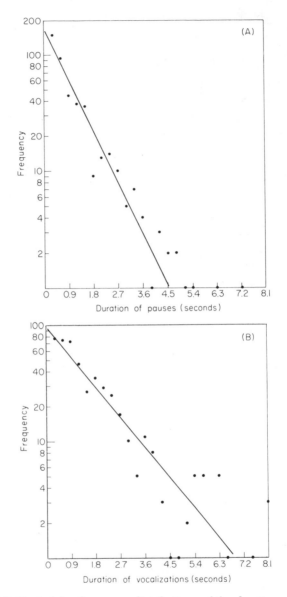

FIGURE II-3. Typical log-frequency distributions of the durations of (A) pauses and (B) vocalizations that occur in a monologue. For each graph the straight line represents the exponential curve based upon the proportionality constant, which is the best fit to the distribution. The distributions are derived from a monologue lasting 20 minutes.

Note that if the brief interjection by speaker B in time unit 10 were subthreshold, that speaker A would have held the floor from units 2 through 17, two speaker switches would not have occurred, both switching pauses would simply be pauses for speaker A, and unit 12 would be reclassified as a vocalization for A and as simultaneous speech for B.

VII. Monologue as a Special Case of Dialogue

It is clear that the preceding set of rules may be applied to un-interrupted monologue as well as to dialogue. However, since all five categories are transactionally defined, a speaker in monologue holds the floor continuously. His speech may contain pauses, but no switching pauses or simultaneous speech. The only discontinuity in description from dialogue to monologue is that certain rubrics cannot occur.

VIII. Distributions of the Categories

The distributions of the classification categories have generally been found to be exponential. Two typical computer-generated frequency histograms for durations of pauses and vocalizations in a monologue are shown in Figures II-3A and B, plotted on semi-log paper. Figure II-4, A–D represents similar graphs for the pauses, vocalizations, switching pauses, and simultaneous speech of a speaker in a dialogue. An exponential curve, plotted on semilog paper, would produce a perfectly straight line. Thus, the degree to which the distributions approximate a straight line reflects the degree to which they are exponentially shaped. With the exception of the tail of the distributions, which represents rather infrequent events, the exponential model seems a good one.

In exponential distributions, based upon discrete sampling inter-vals, the limiting ratio of the frequency of any event of length n to the frequency of length $n - 1$ is a constant which uniquely des-cribes the shape of the curve. It is called the proportionality con-stant and is identical to the probability of continuing the event in

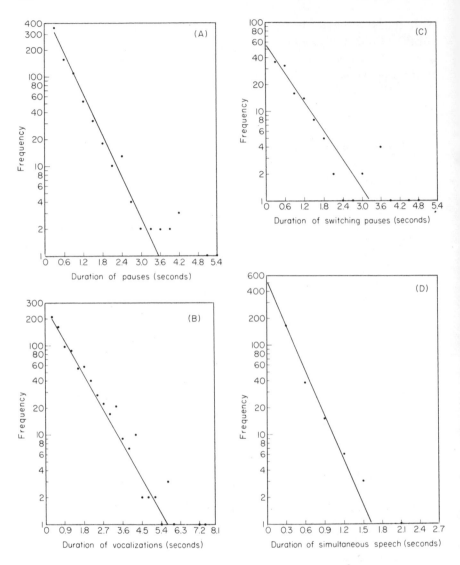

FIGURE II-4. Typical log-frequency distributions of the durations of (A) pauses, (B) vocalizations, (C) switching pauses, and (D) simultaneous speech of speakers in a dialogue. For each graph the straight line represents the exponential curve based upon the proportionality constant, which is the best fit to the distribution. The distributions are derived from a dialogue lasting 50 minutes.

question. Since the vocalization and pause proportionality constants are descriptive of an individual speaker's time domain, they may be interpreted as individual characteristics. They describe a speaker's manner of apportioning the time available to him within the constraints of dialogue.

IX. Extension to Larger Groups

Extension to groups larger than dyads is straightforward, each new speaker adding another voice relay to the system. The pause and vocalization categories would multiply simply by the number of speakers and would describe the time domain of each. However, the number of switching pause states for n speakers would be $n^2 - n$, each with its own distribution. The variety of simultaneous speech states would, of course, multiply at an alarming rate with increase in group size over two. However, as in the case of the reduction of the classification when $n = 1$, no discontinuity in definitions is necessary for expansion to triologues or multilogues.

CHAPTER III

EXPERIMENTAL TESTS OF THE DESCRIPTIVE CLASSIFICATION

Empirically, the division of the vocal energy pattern of conversation into the categories of the descriptive classification seems obvious; they are the commonsense events arrived at by most investigators in this field.

One might question the division of silence into pauses and switching pauses. Are we correct in assuming that gaps in the stream of speech should be classified differently simply because their boundary configurations differ? This is a classic question of taxonomy and the primary purpose of this chapter, which is to determine whether the analysis of actual conversations provides justification for any of the distinctions made by the descriptive classification. To this end, we shall examine (a) the interrelationships among the parameters generated by the distinctions, (b) their reliabilities, and (c) the extent to which they are modifiable. The information pertinent to these issues is compiled from the data of three experiments which have been reported in detail elsewhere. A brief review of the designs of the studies will provide a context for their comparison. Issues (a), (b), and (c) above will then be discussed for the group of experiments as a whole.

I. Designs of the Three Studies

The experiments were conducted in the order in which they are described below. The goals of the research dictated that we control as many of the variables likely to affect the time patterns of interaction as possible, among them age, sex, education, socioeconomic status, nationality, speech pathology, and obvious mental illness. To this end, all subjects in the studies were native born, white students attending colleges in the New York metropolitan area, who volunteered and were paid for their participation. All were free of speech defects and spoke English as their first language.

Inasmuch as it was the initial investigation of the classification categories, the first study (Cassotta, Feldstein, & Jaffe, 1967) sought primarily to answer the question of whether the categories could be considered parameters capable of discriminating among individuals in dyadic verbal interaction. For this reason, an effort was made to control one of the participants in each dyad by using an interview structure and the same interviewers for all subjects. A further question was whether the categories could be considered parameters that, regardless of their ability to differentiate individuals, were modifiable. Could they discriminate different conversational situations? The second and third experiments were also concerned with the reliability and stability of the categories but extended the scope of these concerns in at least two important directions. The second (Feldstein, Jaffe, & Cassotta, 1966, 1967) examined the temporal behavior of individuals in relatively unstructured conversations with different conversational partners. The third added the effects of repeated unstructured conversations by the same pairs of individuals.

Experiment 1. Fifty female subjects, whose ages ranged from 17 to 23 years and averaged 19 years, were interviewed on two separate occasions. On the first occasion, a 16-minute interview was conducted. On the next occasion, approximately two weeks later, three successive 16-minute interviews were conducted, the first by the original interviewer, and the remaining two by another interviewer. The first three interviews dealt essentially with factual biographical information. The content of the fourth, however, was altered in order to provide an opportunity for evaluating the modifiability of the parameters. Specifically, the interviewer questioned the subject in detail about topics which, by her own report, the subject found embarrassing to discuss.

Experiment 2. The second study involved 32 male and 32 female subjects. Their ages ranged from 16 to 37 and averaged 21 years. They were told that the experiment was an investigation of how people attempt to resolve attitudinal differences verbally. Each participant completed a questionnaire (Collins, 1964) concerned with interrracial attitudes; the primary purpose was to provide sufficient material for an extended conversation, and to standardize in a general way the topic discussed. The experimental design called for the participation of each subject in three 40-minute dialogues with another subject at approximately three-week intervals. A subject talked with a member of his own sex on one occasion, a member of the opposite sex on a second occasion, and a different member of his own sex on a third. On each occasion the subjects were instructed to resolve verbally their attitudinal differences as expressed on the questionnaire. In addition, each 40-minute conversation was divided into two conditions. During either the first or second 20 minutes, an opaque screen was placed between the participants in order to eliminate visual–gestural communications and thereby provide the opportunity for further investigating the modifiability of the parameters.

Experiment 3. Twenty-four female subjects participated in Experiment 3. Their ages ranged from 17 to 23 years and averaged 20 years. The subjects were divided into six equal subgroups. The design of the study required that each person in a subgroup converse with every other person in that subgroup for half an hour. Each person, therefore, was paired with three other persons; each subgroup yielded six dyads. To the end of securing more natural social dialogues than were elicited in Experiments 1 and 2, the subjects were instructed to provide their own discussion areas. A small pilot study showed that it was not necessary to provide specific topics in order for active conversations to take place. The participants of each dyad met for eight consecutive half-hour periods of interaction, each scheduled a day apart.

II. Interrelationships of the Categories

In the first study, the temporal parameters were characterized by proportionality constants.[1] In the second and third studies, mean durations of occurrence were used to describe the parameters.

The initial treatment of the data addressed itself to the inter-relations among the parameters. The reason for beginning with such a consideration was that we had no prior empirical evidence that the categories in fact represented independent parameters. Thus, the parameters were compared using product–moment corre-lations. When average correlation coefficients were obtained, they were computed by using z' transformations of the individual coefficients.

Inspection of the data in the first experiment indicated that simultaneous speech occurred too infrequently to permit either an assessment of its reliability or of its relation to the other param-eters. Comparisons were made, therefore, among the other three parameters that were investigated in that experiment, i.e., vocaliza-tions, pauses, and switching pauses.

The interviewees' values of the parameters were intercorrelated for each interview, and an average of the resulting four coefficients for each parameter was obtained. The comparison of pauses and vocalizations yielded an average coefficient of −.47, of switching pauses and vocalizations, −.34. The comparison of pauses and switching pauses yielded a coefficient of .23.

Obviously, the parameters are not all statistically independent of each other. On the other hand, the coefficients are not so high as to preclude the possibility that each parameter may make a unique contribution. What could not be assessed at the conclusion of this first study was the influence of the interview structure upon the relation among the parameters. We shall see shortly that this in-flence was considerable.

In the second experiment, the relations among the parameters were assessed by intercorrelating the average durations of the parameters for all the dyad participants within each of the two conditions on each occasion. Thus, the comparison of any two parameters yielded six coefficients (three occasions each having

---

[1] A proportionality constant (PC) is simply a transformation of the mean (M) such that $PC = (M-1)/M$. The rationale for its use in the first study is presented in the previous chapter.

two conditions). The average of the six coefficients for each comparison is presented in Table III-1. Here we see that, in contrast to the first study, vocalizations are statistically independent of pauses and of switching pauses. Moreover, simultaneous speech (pooled for both speakers), which is now frequent enough to assess, is independent not only of pauses and switching pauses, but also of vocalizations. The relation between pauses and switching pauses, however, is significantly stronger in this than in the previous study.

TABLE III-1

PRODUCT–MOMENT CORRELATION COEFFICIENTS FOR COMPARISONS AMONG PAUSES (P), SWITCHING PAUSES (SP), VOCALIZATIONS (V), AND SIMULTANEOUS SPEECH (SS) AVERAGED OVER THE OCCASIONS AND CONDITIONS OF THE SECOND STUDY[a]

	SP	V	SS
P	.65	−.05	−.07
SP	−	.01	.05
V	−	−	.21

[a] The values used for the correlations were the average durations of each of the parameters. The df for each of the individual comparisons was 60. Averaging of the coefficients was done by using z' transformations. An r of .25 is required for significance at the .05 level (two-tailed).

TABLE III-2

PRODUCT–MOMENT CORRELATION COEFFICIENTS FOR COMPARISONS AMONG PAUSES (P), SWITCHING PAUSES (SP), VOCALIZATIONS (V), SIMULTANEOUS SPEECH (SS), AND SPEAKER SWITCHES (SSW)[a,b]

	SP	V	SS	SSW
P	.60	−.28	−.22	−.26
SP	−	−.24	−.26	−.30
V	−	−	.36	−.10
SS	−	−	−	.19

[a] Averaged over the eight occasions of the third study.
[b] The values used for the comparisons were the average durations of each of the parameters. The df for each comparison is 22. Averaging of the coefficients was done by using z' transformations. An r of .40 is required for significance at the .05 level (two-tailed).

The interrelations among the parameters in Experiment 3 are described in Table III-2. Note that the pattern of relationships among those parameters which concerned us in the second study remains similar in this one. Only the comparison of pauses and switching pauses yielded a significant coefficient. Moreover, the magnitude of the coefficient is similar to its counterpart in the second study.

Earlier in the chapter we questioned the utility of separating pauses and switching pauses. We now discover at least one benefit of the separation; it begins to look as if the magnitude of the relation between pauses and switching pauses differentiates two quite different types of dialogue — the interview and the unconstrained conversation.

III. Parameter Reliabilities

Consider the parameters with respect to four types of reliability: (a) reliability within any single conversation (split-half); (b) stability over time with the same partner; (c) stability as affected by changing conversational partners; and (d) reliability as affected by changing experimental conditions. In talking about these reliabilities, we are actually talking about the consistency of those aspects of an individual's performance that we have elected to examine. We are asking whether his performance can be shown not to vary haphazardly from moment to moment, conversation to conversation, conversational partner to conversational partner, and/or condition to condition.

A. WITHIN A CONVERSATION

Reliabilities for the initial experiment were estimated by computing product–moment correlation coefficients of the interviewees' data for the six possible pairs of the four interviews (Table III-3). There are no unconfounded estimates in this study (or the second one) of the reliabilities of the parameters within a conversation. The reliability estimates for the comparison of interviews one and two are confounded by the time interval between the interviews. Those derived from the comparison of interviews two and three are confounded by a change of interviewer. Finally, interviews three and four represented different conditions. It could, however, be maintained that the change of interviewers may be ignored because all the subjects interacted with each of the two interviewers, and the topical focus of the interviews was similar. An inspection of Table III-3 shows the reliabilities from interview two to interview three to be quite high.

TABLE III-3

PRODUCT–MOMENT CORRELATION COEFFICIENTS FOR THE
SIX POSSIBLE COMPARISONS OF THE FOUR INTERVIEWS (I)
OF THE INITIAL STUDY FOR PAUSES (P), SWITCHING
PAUSES (SP), AND VOCALIZATIONS (V)[a]

		I_2	I_3	I_4
P	I_1	.64	.67	.58
	I_2	–	.80	.70
	I_3	–	–	.67
SP	I_1	.53	.43	.46
	I_2	–	.62	.41
	I_3	–	–	.36
V	I_1	.61	.57	.40
	I_2	–	.81	.61
	I_3	–	–	.68

[a] The proportionality constants of P, SP, and V were used in calculating the coefficients. The df for each r is 48. The average of the six coefficients for each parameter is .68 for pauses, .49 for switching pauses, and .62 for vocalizations. A coefficient of .28 is required for significance at the .05 level (two-tailed).

In the second experiment, the 40-minute dialogues that took place on each of the three occasions were divided into two 20-minute conditions, a vis-a-vis condition and a screen condition. The stabilities of the parameters from one condition to the other will be examined shortly in another section.

It is only Experiment 3 that provides unconfounded estimates of the speakers' consistency within a conversation. In processing the 30-minute dialogues of the third study, we divided each into two 15-minute segments and computed the parameter values for each segment. The average durations of the parameters for the two segments of each occasion were correlated, and the coefficients presented in Table III-4 were obtained. As can be seen, the average reliabilities of the parameters are quite comparable to those obtained in the first study. The same level of reliability was achieved by even the two parameters (simultaneous speech and speaker

TABLE III-4

PRODUCT–MOMENT CORRELATION COEFFICIENTS FOR THE COMPARISON OF THE
FIRST AND SECOND FIFTEEN-MINUTE SEGMENTS WITHIN EACH OCCASION
OF THE THIRD STUDY FOR PAUSES (P), SWITCHING PAUSES (SP),
VOCALIZATIONS (V), SIMULTANEOUS SPEECH (SS),
AND SPEAKER SWITCHING (SSW)[a]

Parameter	Occasions								Average
	1	2	3	4	5	6	7	8	
P	.76	.78	.64	.66	.66	.77	.69	.67	.71
SP	.61	.72	.65	.76	.70	.72	.79	.79	.72
V	.86	.79	.79	.42	.77	.72	.84	.76	.76
SS	.52	.30	.40	.74	.47	.40	.48	.75	.53
SSW	.69	.56	.54	.54	.75	.57	.64	.69	.63

[a] The values used for the correlations were the average durations of all the parameters except SSW (which could only be frequencies). The df for each comparison is 22. A coefficient of .40 is required for significance at the .05 level (two-tailed).

switches) not examined in that study. It seems safe at this point to conclude that the categories of the descriptive classification yield values that remain highly stable during the course of a conversation. Thus, one may also conclude that, as suggested earlier, the categories do indeed describe behavior patterns that are characteristic of individuals in conversation.

B. OVER TIME

The first and second interviews of Experiment 1 used the same interviewer and the same general content, but were separated by about two weeks. A comparison of the two interviews, however, yielded parameter reliabilities not significantly higher or lower than those obtained from a comparison of the second and third interviews and third and fourth interviews (Table III-3). It appears as if the stability of the parameters over time is at least as high as it is at any particular time. The reliability estimates derived from comparisons among the three occasions in the second study cannot be considered primarily as measures of stability over time, because they confound the three-week time interval with the effects of different conversational partners.

Intercorrelations among the eight occasions of the third study do represent stability estimates over time, but it must be remembered that between the first and eighth occasion, for example, were seven other occasions. The average of the 28 estimates[2] for each parameter is .65 for pauses, .66 for switching pauses, .68 for vocalizations, .30 for simultaneous speech, and .61 for number of speaker switches. These estimates provide further evidence that, with the exception of simultaneous speech, those components of conversational time patterns that we have chosen to investigate are remarkably stable over time and, indeed, over many conversations of the same speaker. Even a comparison of the first and eighth occasions yields stability estimates of .40 for pauses, .52 for switching pauses, .62 for vocalizations, and .72 for speaker switching. These are quite similar to the average estimates of the 28 comparisons. On the other hand, the extent to which conversationalists talk at the same time is consistent only during a single conversation. There is no evidence that two speakers develop a characteristic duration of talking simultaneously which remains stable over many of their conversations.

C. DIFFERENT CONVERSATIONAL PARTNERS

The designs of Experiments 2 and 3 allowed for the best estimates of the effect of changing conversational partners upon parameter reliabilities. While it is true that there were two interviewers in Experiment 1, they comprised the "other speaker" in all of the interviews. In the second and third studies, however, each speaker conversed with three different speakers, and no two individuals had the same conversational partner on any one occasion. For the second study, product–moment correlation coefficients were computed for comparisons among the three occasions, and the averages of these coefficients are .29 for pauses, .30 for switching pauses,

---

[2] There are 28 possible comparisons among the eight occasions.

.47 for vocalizations, and .27 for simultaneous speech. Changing conversational partners obviously had a marked effect, although the resulting reliability coefficients are still significantly different from zero. This decreased stability suggests that the temporal patterns of an individual's conversational style vary as a function of the temporal pattern of the person with whom he converses. This effect was assessed in the third study by comparing the parameter values obtained by the subjects in interaction with one set of partners to those obtained by the subjects in interaction with each of their two other sets of partners on each occasion. Here we find (Table III-5) that the influence of the partners' temporal styles upon those of the speakers was apparently so marked that the latter could not remain stable from partner to partner. The one component of temporal style that did maintain its stability is vocalizations. This exception suggests that the characteristic duration of an individual's vocalizations does not readily yield to the influence of other speakers' temporal styles.

Why should there be a difference in the degree of this type of

TABLE III-5

AVERAGE PRODUCT–MOMENT CORRELATION COEFFICIENTS FOR
COMPARISONS AMONG THE TIME PATTERNS OF THE SUBJECTS
IN THEIR INTERACTION WITH THREE SETS OF PARTNERS ON EACH
OCCASION OF THE THIRD STUDY[a]

Parameter	Occasions								Average
	1	2	3	4	5	6	7	8	
P	.28	.30	.34	.40	.30	.43	.26	.33	.33
SP	.29	.32	.27	.41	.27	.40	.35	.28	.33
V	.73	.78	.68	.58	.72	.69	.76	.81	.72
SS	.27	−.02	−.03	.12	.30	−.04	.31	.06	.12
SSW	.15	.05	−.01	.20	.26	.22	.27	.10	.16

[a] P stands for pauses, SP for switching pauses, V for vocalizations, SS for simultaneous speech, and SSW for speaker switches. Each coefficient is the average of the three coefficients computed for each occasion. The values used for the correlations were the average durations of all the parameters other than SSW (which could only be frequencies). The df for each comparison was 22. A coefficient of .40 is required for significance at the .05 level (two-tailed).

reliability from Experiments 2 to 3? One possible explanation may have to do with the topics of the conversations in the two studies. In the second, all conversations, regardless of partner, were by design concerned with the same content. In the third, the subjects were encouraged to discuss whatever topics they wished and were free to change them, not only from one partner to the next, but even with the same partner on different occasions. It may well have been this combination of a change in partners and a change in discussion content that destroyed the stability of the speakers' temporal patterns.

D. DIFFERENT CONDITIONS

We had introduced into the first and second experiments a change in some aspect of the condition under which the conversations occurred in order to investigate the modifiability of temporal patterning in dyadic verbal interaction. In the initial study, the topic of the fourth interview was appreciably altered, whereas, in the second study, the placing of an opaque screen between the speakers effectively deleted visual–gestural communication from the interaction. We shall shortly explore the effects of these condition changes upon the parameter values. Here, however, we want to explore the stability of the conversationalists' temporal patterns as affected by the condition change. Table III-3 indicates that the comparison of interviews three and four yielded stability estimates for the parameters that are all significantly different from zero. The estimate for pauses is .67, for switching pauses is .36, and for vocalizations is .68. In the second study, the average stability estimates resulting from a comparison of the vis-a-vis and screen conditions on each occasion are .67 for pauses, .68 for switching pauses, .66 for vocalizations, and .53 for simultaneous speech. There is no astounding difference between the first three estimates and their counterparts in the second study. Both sets suggest that however these condition changes affected the absolute parameter values, they had little effect upon the consistency with which speakers maintained their temporal styles from one condition to the other.

In summary, the results of the three experiments suggest that the time patterns of an individual's conversational style—the duration of his pauses, his switching pauses, his vocalizations, and his contribution to the frequency of speaker switches in a conversation — remain markedly stable during the course of a conversation and consistent from one conversation to another with the same partner regardless of the time lapse between them, or whether the topical focus or some other condition of the conversations changes.

Another important implication of the reliabilities obtained in these studies is that there are discernible, stable interindividual differences in the organizing of conversational time. There are, for example, individuals whose pauses are characteristically longer than those of other individuals, and they tend to remain longer in a variety of circumstances. This does not necessarily mean that the pause durations of such individuals remain the same in different situations, but simply that they retain the same or similar rank relative to the pause durations of other individuals. Whether, in fact, the parameter values do vary systematically from one situation to another is a question of importance equal to that concerning their reliability.

IV. Modifiability of the Parameters

It is not ordinarily obvious that people may be characterized by the timing of their conversational interactions. True, there are exceptions; the person "who never lets you get a word in edgewise" is one. Pressed to consider it, most of us would tend to ascribe responsibility for the time patterns of a conversation to a host of factors other than individual consistency, such as the topic under discussion, the feelings of the participants, their opinions of each other, and the physical context in which the conversation occurs. Moreover, it is most probable that these factors do indeed affect the flow of a conversation. Our concern in this section is whether the parameters defined by the descriptive classification are capable of reflecting the impact of different conversational conditions, in short, whether the parameters are modifiable.

We have shown that the temporal styles of individuals in conversation remain stable despite the introduction of embarrassing, perhaps stressful, topics into the discussion. We have also shown that this stability persists even in the face of a total loss of visual–

gestural information during a conversation. We might now examine these conditions in greater detail in order to look at the discernible effects upon temporal patterning that were associated with them. It should be emphasized that we shall here view the two conditions simply as opportunities for testing the modifiability of the parameters.

A. EFFECTS OF STRESS

The design of the fourth interview in the initial study permitted an investigation of the relation between temporal patterning and induced stress. As a matter of fact, the interview represented an effort to provide greater generality of the reliability estimates by introducing a topical focus that was markedly different from that of the first three interviews. The subject matter of these three interviews was the quite familiar information about educational history, personal interests, general attitudes, etc. By contrast, the fourth interview was designed to elicit information of an intimate, embarrassing nature (Cassotta *et al.*, 1967, p. 9). The success of this maneuver was inferred from the subjects' reports and from a comparison of their speech during this, the fourth interview, with their speech during the third interview. The comparison involved a lexical measure of speech fluency called the Speech Disturbance Ratio (Mahl, 1959) which has been related to momentary changes in anxiety level. It was found that the interviewees' speech was significantly more disrupted during the fourth than during the third interview.

Analyses of the proportionality constants (see footnote 1) of pauses, switching pauses,[3] and vocalizations indicated that little change in the average duration of vocalizations had occurred from the third to the fourth interview. The average durations of the interviewees' pauses and switching pauses, however, were significantly longer and shorter, respectively, in the fourth than in the third interview. In other words, the presumably increased stress of the

---

[3]The switching pauses used in the analysis presented here were defined according to the classification described in the previous chapter. In the original study (Cassotta *et al.*, 1967), however, the switching pauses of the interviewees were defined as those silences which *preceded* (rather than followed) their utterances and were conceived of as latencies or response times.

interviewees was associated with marked increases in the duration of silences within the flow of their speech and marked decreases in the duration of silences that signaled the interaction of the interviewer.

This increase in pause duration suggests that the interviewees were to some extent less willing or able to sustain the dialogue in the stress interview than they were in the nonstress interview. The decrease in the duration of switching pauses suggests that the pace of the interaction changed as a function of the stress. (See Table D-1, Appendix D, for descriptive statistics.)

A certain reservation should be mentioned here which may bear upon the degree to which these findings would obtain in an "ordinary" conversation in which one or both of the participants are under stress. Although the general format of both the third and fourth interviews was similar, the former utilized a preformulated questionnaire, whereas in the latter, the interviewer played it by ear. Thus, the latter was a less structured exchange. The effects of stress and format are, therefore, somewhat confounded in the comparison of the two interviews.[4] The important point for our present purposes, however, is that the change of condition represented by the fourth interview was reflected by significant changes in the values of two of the three temporal parameters examined. These changes provide some evidence that the parameters are modifiable.

B. LOSS OF VISUAL–GESTURAL CUES

Further evidence attesting to the modifiability of the parameters was provided by the second study. As stated earlier, the two conditions of the second study were the ordinary face-to-face (or vis-á-vis) conversation and a conversation during which all visual-gestural information was eliminated (called the "screen" condition). Apart from viewing the screen condition as simply another test of parameter modifiability, we were, of course, interested in whether the lack of any visual–gestural cues would have a discernible im-

---

[4] It may be that the questions in the fourth interview were more ambiguous than those in the third and that this ambiguity, rather than the inferred state of stress, was responsible for the resulting differences between the two interviews (e.g., Siegman & Pope, 1965).

pact upon the temporal pattern of a conversation. It did seem likely that such cues are used by each participant in a conversation to evaluate the ongoing interaction and to guide, thereby, the content and form of his continuing participation.

The raw data were analyzed in terms of vocalizations, pauses, switching pauses, and simultaneous speech. The values of these parameters were subjected to separate analyses of variance for each occasion. In the analyses of the first three parameters, the sex of the subjects and the order in which they participated in the two conversational conditions represented independent sources of variance as did the interaction of sex and order. The two conditions and their interactions with sex and order represented dependent sources of variance. Inasmuch as simultaneous speech was treated as a dyadic parameter (i.e., each member of a conversation is credited with the same duration of simultaneous speech), its analysis investigated the variance associated with the sex of the dyads (i.e., male–male, female–female, or male–female), rather than the sex of the subjects. Unfortunately, no direct comparisons among the occasions could be made because the order in which the subjects participated in the two conditions was not the same from occasion to occasion.

The significant sources of variance associated with the comparison of the vis-à-vis and screen conditions for each analysis are presented in Table III-6. The differences in the vocal behavior of the subjects between the vis-à-vis and screen conditions noticeably accounted for a significant portion of the variance, either alone or in interaction with the differences engendered by the order in which the conditions occurred and, at times by the sex of the subjects or dyads. (See Tables D-2 to D-5 of Appendix D for descriptive statistics.)

The results suggest that when faced with the loss of visual–gestural cues, conversationalists often tend to alter the temporal patterning of their interaction, and that the sex of the conversationalists and the point in the interaction at which the loss occurs contribute to the alterations. When effective by itself (i.e., as a main effect), the lack of visual–gestural information was associated with relatively shorter durations of pauses, switching pauses, and simultaneous speech. It may be that the shorter bursts of simultaneous speech represent caution. It is more difficult, however, to account for the shorter durations of pauses and switching pauses. One might

TABLE III-6

SIGNIFICANT SOURCES OF VARIANCE ASSOCIATED WITH THE ANALYSES OF THE CONDITION EFFECTS UPON PAUSES (P), SWITCHING PAUSES (SP), VOCALIZATIONS (V), AND SIMULTANEOUS SPEECH (SS), FOR EACH OCCASION OF THE SECOND STUDY[a]

Occasion	P			SP			V			SS		
	Source	df	F	Source	df	F	Source	df	F	Source	df	F
First same sex	(C×O	1,60	3.15)	C	1,60	5.57	(C	1,60	3.5)	—	—	—
	C×O×S	1,60	7.73	C×O×S	1,60	4.55	C×O	1,60	5.00	—	—	—
Second same sex	—	—	—	—	—	—	—	—	—	—	—	—
							(C	1,58	3.75)	C	1,27	20.04
										(C	1,29	3.15)
Mixed sex	C	1,58	7.53	C	1,58	15.61	—	—	—	—	—	—
	(C×O×S	1,58	2.82)	—								

[a] C stands for conditions and refers to the vis-à-vis and screen conditions, O for the order in which the conditions occurred, and S for the sex of the subjects. The F ratios in parentheses have a p value between the .05 and .10 levels of significance (two-tailed). The remaining F ratios are significant beyond the .05 and .01 levels. The amount of variance each of the sources accounts for can be estimated with the formula, $(F - 1) df_1 / (F\, df_1 + df_2)$, where df_1 is the degrees of freedom associated with the numerator of the F ratio, and df_2 is the degrees of freedom associated with the denominator.

conjecture that, in the absence of visual information to serve as a guide, silences in conversation become, like "dead time" on a telephone or radio, peaks of uncertainty and, thus, difficult to sustain. The significant interactions of conditions with sex and order are the most difficult to interpret. Apparently, sudden access to the visual–gestural channel after a period of conversing in its absence precipitated marked changes in certain aspects of vocal behavior. On the other hand, the influence of gender appears to have been inconsistent.

In any case, the pertinent aspect of these findings with regard to our concern here is that they further confirm the modifiability of the parameter values. The conditions of this and the previous experiments were distinctly different. That they affected the time patterns of the subjects' conversations enhances the possibility that the patterns are systematically sensitive to a variety of changes in the circumstances of conversation. Another such change involves varying conversational partners. We noted earlier that the parameter values of conversationalists appear to remain stable even though their partners change from one conversation to another. We also noted, however, that this stability was less than that resulting from repeated conversations with the same partner. We shall now examine the influence that seems to account for the decreased stability.

C. INTERSPEAKER INFLUENCE

It seems eminently reasonable to expect that the participants in a conversation influence each other's ways of speaking. This influence undoubtedly extends even to the words that are used. It also appears to extend to aspects of the nonlexical structure of interaction.

There are a number of ways of assessing interspeaker influence. In the initial study, for example, we might intercorrelate the parameter values obtained by the *interviewers* in each of the four interviews. Inasmuch as there were only two interviewers, each of whom talked to all the interviewees, significant correlation coefficients among the interviews would indicate that the interviewers' conversational styles were influenced by those of the interviewees, i.e., that the interviewers' styles tended to differ with different interviewees and that the difference persisted from interview to interview. It turns out that correlations of the interviewers' data, averaged over interview pairs[5] and over the interviewers, yielded coefficients of .29 for pauses, .60 for switching pauses, and .16 for vocalizations. It begins to appear as if the silences within a dialogue, at least within a dialogue as highly structured as the interviews of this study, are quite susceptible to interspeaker influence, particularly those silences that intervene between the utterances of the two speakers. It also seems, as was suggested earlier, as if vocalizations—the duration of speech bursts that people utilize in conversing—may not be too susceptible.

D. Effect on Multiple Partners

A similar approach to the assessment of interspeaker influence involves an examination of the consistency with which the temporal style of one speaker affects the styles of other speakers with whom he interacts. The rationale is that if the temporal style of a speaker is able to influence the styles of those with whom he converses, then those styles ought to resemble each other somewhat.

In the second study, each subject spoke with three other subjects who, for convenience, we might call partners. Comparisons among the parameter values of the three sets of partners yielded average product–moment correlation coefficients of .39 for pauses, .37 for switching pauses, and .11 for vocalizations. It should be noted that these are somewhat confounded estimates, i.e., there was an interval of about two weeks between the conversations of the subjects with each of their partners. In the third study, each subject talked with three other subjects, or partners, on each of the eight occasions. Table III-7 presents the results of the comparisons among the scores of the three partners on each occasion. (See Table D-6 of Appendix D for descriptive statistics.)

Whereas in the second study the speakers apparently influenced the durations of their partners' silences, there was no evidence of such influence in the third study. There was little similarity among the partners in the way they paced their interactions with the subjects. This result supports the finding, reported earlier, that there was no consistent effect by the subjects upon the temporal

---

[5] Excluded from these averages were the coefficients resulting from the comparison of data from interviews three and four.

TABLE III-7

AVERAGE PRODUCT–MOMENT CORRELATION COEFFICIENTS FOR COMPARISONS
AMONG THE TIME PATTERNS OF THE THREE SETS OF PARTNERS IN THEIR
INTERACTION WITH THE SUBJECTS ON EACH OCCASION OF THE THIRD STUDY[a]

Parameter	Occasions								Average
	1	2	3	4	5	6	7	8	
P	.13	.11	.11	.20	.21	.26	.39	.51	.24
SP	.12	.03	.32	.13	.06	.22	.36	.31	.20
V	.13	.26	.27	.41	.18	.22	.38	.38	.28

[a] P stands for pauses, SP for switching pauses, and V for vocalizations. (Inasmuch as simultaneous speech and speaker switches are dyadic parameters, correlations among the partners' scores are the same as correlations among the scores made by the subjects in interaction with the three sets of partners. The latter are presented in Table III-5. Each coefficient is the average of the three coefficients computed for each occasion. The values used for the correlations were the average durations of all the parameters. The df for each comparison was 22. A coefficient of .40 is required for significance at the .05 level (two-tailed).

styles of their three partners. As we suggested when we discussed this lack of reliability, the free choice of topics may have played a much more potent role than was expected.

E. CONGRUENCE

A more direct way to assess interspeaker influence is to compare the average parameter values of one participant in a dyad with those of the other participant over many dyads and for those parameters for which such a comparison is feasible. Obviously, comparisons of simultaneous speech and speaker switches would be meaningless because both participants in a dyad are assigned the same values. We might, for ease of reference, call the correlation coefficients resulting from such comparisons coefficients of congruence. The term congruence is used because the coefficient is an index of the degree to which the interacting speakers tend to match the temporal patterning of each other's speech, i.e., to achieve similarity. Note that this coefficient is computed over many dyads and is not concerned with the moment-to-moment tracking of each participant by the other *within* a particular conversation. We shall return shortly to a consideration of the latter type of behavior.

Comparisons of the interviewees' data with those of the interviewers' yielded average congruence coefficients of .39 for pauses, .42 for switching pauses, and .32 for vocalizations. While the three coefficients are significant, they are relatively low, probably because the same interviewers interacted with all the subjects. In the second study, in which the participants of the dyads were all different within each occasion, the intraclass[6] coefficients of congruence, averaged over occasions and conditions, were .56 for pauses, .55 for switching pauses, and a nonsignificant −.04 for vocalizations. Here we see that in the relatively unstructured conversations of the second experiment, speakers were unable to influence the durations of each other's vocalizations. That this was not the case in the initial study may reflect the role differences between interviewers and interviewees, the fact that the interviewees all spoke to the same interviewers, or the different interactional rules of an interview. Nevertheless, the coefficients of congruence that were obtained suggest that a considerable degree of pattern matching took place in the dialogues of both studies.[7]

Comparisons of the parameter values of the dyad participants in

---

[6] Intraclass rather than product–moment correlations were used because of the lack of explicit role differences between the participants of each dyad. Thus, whether the parameter value of a conversationalist fell into the x or y column of a comparison was purely arbitrary. The significance of an intraclass correlation coefficient is determined by the F test associated with the intraclass analysis of variance (Haggard, 1958).

[7] The assessment of pattern matching (congruence) could be extended to include more than one conversation by the same speakers. One approach to such an assessment would be to (a) obtain the differences between the parameter values of the two speakers for each dialogue, and (b) evaluate the direction and strength of these differences from the initial to the final dialogue (e.g., by a trend analysis). One would want this analysis to reveal whether the parameter values of the speakers converged or diverged by the final dialogue. To do so properly, however, the analysis must take into account the starting point, or initial difference, of the trend. Obviously, convergence, or a decreasing difference over dialogues, cannot be demonstrated for a set of differences having an initial value of zero. We have not yet solved this problem of accounting for initial value to our satisfaction. A preliminary analysis of the differences for the eight occasions of Experiment 3 yielded a significant linear component of divergence for vocalizations and for switching pauses, and no significant trend for pauses. Another study (Welkowitz & Feldstein, 1969), concerned with the effect of perceived interpersonal similarity upon dialogic time patterns, showed significant linear convergence over the course of three dialogues for vocalizations and switching pauses and, again, no significant trend for pauses. Neither study, however, took the initial value into account in its analyses of the differences.

the third study yielded results that essentially replicate those of the second. Inspection of Table III-8 indicates that the speakers influenced the durations of each other's pauses and switching pauses to a significant degree, whereas they were unable to affect the durations of each other's vocalizations. It might be surmised that, inasmuch as speakers achieved relatively similar degrees of congruence in both the second and third studies, the topical focus of a conversation exerts relatively little effect on pattern matching. On the other hand, the foci of exchanges in both studies were, for the most part, presumably inoffensive. The findings do not rule out the possibility that pattern matching would not occur in angry, embittered interactions.

TABLE III-8

AVERAGE COEFFICIENTS OF CONGRUENCE FOR PAUSES (P),
SWITCHING PAUSES (SP), AND VOCALIZATIONS (V)
ON EACH OCCASION OF THE THIRD STUDY[a]

Parameter	Occasions								Over occasions
	1	2	3	4	5	6	7	8	
P	.51	.40	.23	.53	.21	.41	.53	.53	.43
SP	.63	.62	.53	.76	.54	.55	.65	.66	.62
V	.04	.14	.19	.17	−.01	−.01	.10	.02	.08

[a] The coefficients of each occasion are the average of three intraclass correlation coefficients (R) indexing the degree of congruence achieved by the subjects with each of their three sets of partners. The statistical significance of an R is determined by the significance of its associated F ratio (Haggard, 1958). None of the vocalization Rs in the table is significant. Of the remaining Rs, only the .21 for pauses on occasion 5 is of doubtful significance inasmuch as two of the three Fs associated with it were nonsignificant.

F. MOMENT-TO-MOMENT MATCHING

Let us turn briefly to our earlier reference to moment-to-moment tracking of each speaker by the other speaker in a dialogue. To investigate this type of pattern matching, correlations were obtained between the utterance durations used by the two participants in each of eight of the conversations recorded in the second

study (Feldstein, 1968). Because the temporal durations of the individual utterances in these comparisons were unavailable, the
length of each was defined by its number of words. None of the
eight coefficients was even close to the required significance level.
The finding is suggestive but not conclusive. It may indeed be that
such utterance-by-utterance tracking does not occur in relatively
unstructured conversation. Or it may simply be that the finding is a
function of the utterance definition. That is, excluding the durations of pauses from the utterances may have excluded the temporal
element of an utterance most subject to moment-to-moment influence. Considering the relative unsusceptibility of vocalizations
to interspeaker influence, the latter explanation deserves serious
exploration. The same criticism may be made of the results of Ray
and Webb (1966) who, using the number of typewritten lines as
their index of length, failed to find evidence of moment-to-moment
tracking in the question-and-answer press conferences of the late
President Kennedy.

V. Silence and Syntax

There is, however, a more theoretical concern of some importance. This concern has to do with the relation between temporal
style and syntactic structure and their role (or roles) in interactive
behavior. An example of one approach to an aspect of this concern
is a preliminary study (Gerstman, Feldstein, & Jaffe, 1967) which
utilized conversations from the second study described earlier. The
intent of the study was to examine the relative importance of silence
and syntax as cues to speaker switching in spontaneous dialogue.
Fifteen minutes from each of four conversations provided the data
for the study. The data were silences within the flow of speech (no
distinction was made between pauses and switching pauses) and
boundary markings (points of linguistically permissible phrase
endings) on 10,642 words of text transcribed from the 60 minutes of
conversation. The boundary markings were made by each of two
linguists who worked independently and achieved a high degree
of reliability. Inspection of the data revealed that speaker switching
occurred approximately nine times more often after words followed
by a silence than after words not followed by a silence, and approximately 21 times more often after boundaries than after nonbound-

aries. Synchronization of the two data domains indicated that the two effects were nonadditive, that the co-occurrence of both cues made switching 42 times more probable than the co-occurrence of neither. At the same time, switching occurred 2.6 times more frequently after boundary words that were not followed by a silence than after nonboundary words that were followed by a silence. It is not surprising that the syntactic boundary is a stronger determinant of speaker switching than is silence since, at the least, it combines the effects not only of structure but of intonation contour, which is in all likelihood a quite effective determinant in its own right. Of greater importance is the fact that the combination of boundary and silence is considerably more effective than either is alone.

Strictly speaking, our use of the terms "determinant" and "cue" is somewhat presumptuous. It implies an inference from the relationship of boundaries and silences to speaker switching that properly must be tested experimentally. There is one finding of the study that suggests, at least with regard to silence, that the inference would be verified. The more prolonged a silence became, the greater became the probability that it would be succeeded by a speaker switch. It is not surprising that silence itself may have cue value in a conversational exchange. It already has been shown on a microlinguistic level (Baumrin, 1969; Liberman, Harris, Eimas, Lisker, & Bastian, 1961) that the duration of intersyllabic silence markedly affects the identification (communication) of certain phonemes.

The results presented in this chapter suggest that, on the gross level with which we deal, the manipulation of time in conversational interactions offers a viable channel of interpersonal communication. There is no doubt that, within or without awareness, it is recognized and used as such. What remains to be specified is the type of information transmitted by it that differs from and/or complements that of the lexical channel.

CHAPTER IV

STOCHASTIC MODELS OF THE TIME
PATTERNS OF DIALOGUE

In this chapter several mathematical models are proposed
which are somewhat farther from the commonsense perception of
the time sequence of conversation. They are made possible by the
analog to digital conversion of the durations of sound and silence.
Vocal interaction is sampled at fixed intervals and each sample is
uniquely classified into one of four states. This is illustrated extensively later in the chapter. For the present, it is merely asserted
that after a large number of such samples, a probability may be
assigned to each state of the system and to the transitions between
states. This permits the testing of stochastic models of the process,
i.e., models that depend upon a random or chance element.

I. Time Patterns of Monologue

Let us begin with an examination of the uninterrupted monologue of a single speaker to illustrate in a special case the mathematical notions that will be used in the subsequent consideration
of dialogue. The latter will then follow naturally. Recall that the
microphone actuates a voice relay which is closed when the speaker
vocalizes and open when he is silent.[1] The AVTA system inquires
into the state of this voice relay 200 times per minute and classifies
each sample as either silence (state 0) or sound (state 1). Thus, the
raw data for monologue can be regarded simply as a sequence of

---

[1] Details of the AVTA system and its operation are found in Appendix A.

51

zeros and ones. If adjacent samples are found to be in the identical state, that state is assumed to have been continuous in the interval between inquiries. Once the relay is closed by a sound above the threshold setting of the instrument, it will not discriminate a louder from a softer vocalization. We are concerned here merely with presence versus absence of sound and not with intensity fluctuations.

The string of 200 zeros and ones shown in Figure IV-1 represents one minute of hypothetical monologue as encoded by AVTA. In practice, one would require a much longer time series in order to examine probabilistic models, but this sequence serves as a manageable example.

111111111000111111111111111111111111111111111111111111111111111111

11111111111000000000000000001111111111111111111111111111111111100111

1111111111111100111111111111111111111111111111111110100000001111111

FIGURE IV-1. A one-minute sequence of the sounds (1) and silences (0) of a hypothetical monologue as encoded by AVTA.

A count indicates that there are 31 zeros and 169 ones. In the second chapter, runs of silence and sound were treated in the most intuitive way, i.e., as alternating pauses and sound bursts. The durations of each were plotted as pause and vocalization histograms, respectively. These graphs of frequency versus duration were seen to be exponentially distributed. An alternative approach to such a sequence is to construct the transition table, or matrix, shown in Figure IV-2. This is a somewhat less intuitive method of organizing and reducing the data.

In this matrix, each element is the frequency with which a state of sound or silence at time t was followed immediately by a state of sound or silence at time $t + 1$. Since we proceed by single steps, this is a one-step or first-order transition matrix. For example, the sequence 101000 contains the following transitions: 1 to 0, 0 to 1, 1 to 0, 0 to 0, and finally, 0 to 0. If the sequence remains in the same state in successive time units it is considered to have made a transi-

State at time $t+1$

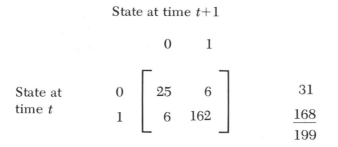

FIGURE IV-2. A one-step transition matrix of the sounds (1) and silences (0) of the one minute of monologue depicted in Figure IV-1.

tion from the state to itself. Note that each digit is considered twice, first as the state at time $t+1$, and then as the state at time t. The first and last of the series can only participate in one transition each, so for k consecutive states there are $k-1$ one-step transitions. Thus, for the 200 states the table shows a total of 199 transitions. The marginals on the right are the row sums, i.e., the absolute number of time units in which sound or silence occurred. Note that the column sums of Table IV-1 could just as well have been used to derive the absolute frequency of each state from the tabulation of one-step transitions. The frequency transition matrix is symmetric, which merely says that the number of changes of state in a two-state system must balance. By convention, the rows of the transition matrix are designated the starting state of each transition at time t, the columns being the outcome state at time $t+1$.

The column of row sums, or marginals, may be normalized by dividing each element by the total number of time units. The resultant vector, symbolized by the capital letter V, is the probability distribution of the two states. $p(i)$ is the notation for the probability of state i, and in this example, i is either 0 or 1. For the sample matrix in Figure IV-2,

$$V = \begin{bmatrix} p(0) \\ p(1) \end{bmatrix} = \begin{bmatrix} .16 \\ .84 \end{bmatrix}$$

The elements of V are absolute probabilities, i.e., the proportion of time units of the monologue, regardless of their locations in the sequence, which are assigned to a particular state. $p(0)$ and $p(1)$ must sum to unity. In symbols,

$$\sum_i p(i) = 1$$

V is a column vector and its transpose, a row vector, is symbolized by V'.

$$V' = [p(0), p(1)] = [.16, .84] \tag{1}$$

This vector of absolute state probabilities is also the stationary distribution of the transition matrix, a point which will be quite important later in this chapter.

The 2 by 2 matrix of transition frequencies in Figure IV-2 is similarly normalized by dividing each of its row frequencies by the respective row sum. This yields a matrix, symbolized by the capital letter P, the elements of which are called sequential, transitional, or conditional probabilities. The subscripted notation used here is p_{ij}, which is the probability of being in state j at time $t+1$ given that we are in state i at time t.

$$P = \begin{bmatrix} p_{00} & p_{01} \\ p_{10} & p_{11} \end{bmatrix}$$

Equation (2) below results when this normalization is performed upon the matrix of transition frequencies shown in Figure IV-2.

$$P = \begin{bmatrix} .81 & .19 \\ .04 & .96 \end{bmatrix} \qquad \begin{matrix} \text{Row Sum} \\ 1.00 \\ 1.00 \end{matrix} \tag{2}$$

Observe that each row of the matrix is now a probability vector giving the distribution of the possible outcomes of a transition from state i. For example, of all the transitions beginning in state 0, 81% ended in state 0 while 19% ended in state 1. Similarly, of the transitions from state 1, 4% ended in state 0 and 96% in state 1. P is therefore a *stochastic matrix*, which is defined as a matrix of nonnegative real numbers such that the sum of the terms in each row is 1. In symbols,

$$\sum_j p_{ij} = 1 \tag{3}$$

Note also that the elements p_{ij} are different from the absolute probability of an ij transition, for which our notation is $p(ij)$. The latter would be obtained by dividing each cell frequency by the total number of transitions in the whole matrix rather than by the respective row sum. In symbols,

$$\sum_{ij} p(ij) = 1 \tag{4}$$

The absolute transition probabilities, $p(ij)$, the conditional transition probabilities, p_{ij}, and the state probabilities, $p(i)$, are related by Equation (5) as follows:

$$p(ij) = p(i)p_{ij} \tag{5}$$

Equation (5) is important for it is central to the prediction of sound and silence histograms later in this chapter. It asserts that the absolute probability of a sequence of two states is the product of the absolute probability of the starting state and the conditional probability given that starting state. It also says that the p_{ij} of our stochastic matrix can be obtained by dividing the absolute probability of an ij transition by the absolute probability of state i.

In symbols,

$$p_{ij} = \frac{p(ij)}{p(i)} \qquad\qquad (6)$$

Multiplying both numerator and denominator of the fraction in Equation (6) by the total number of time units makes this expression equivalent to the division of the frequency of an ij transition by the frequency of state i. Recall that this was the method used to obtain stochastic matrix P from Table IV-1 [Equation (2)].

To summarize the notation to this point, for monologue:

$p(0)$ = absolute probability of silence
$p(1)$ = absolute probability of sound

$p(00)$ = absolute probability of silence following silence
$p(01)$ = absolute probability of sound following silence
$p(10)$ = absolute probability of silence following sound
$p(11)$ = absolute probability of sound following sound

p_{00} = conditional probability of silence following silence
p_{01} = conditional probability of sound following silence
p_{10} = conditional probability of silence following sound
p_{11} = conditional probability of sound following sound

There are two additional ways of visualizing the process described by the stochastic matrix P of Equation (2) and its stationary distribution (vector of state probabilities) as given in Equation (1). The first is known as a state diagram (Figure IV-3). The circles depict the states, and the arrows the two possible transitions from each, i.e., to the other state and back to itself. The indicated transition probabilities from a given state sum to 1.0 and are identical with the associated row vector of matrix P. If this stochastic process ran for a long time, one would expect the absolute proportion of time units spent in each of the states to be given by the stationary distribution, V.

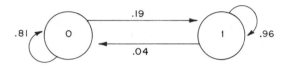

FIGURE IV-3. A state diagram of the conditional probabilities of Equation (2).

Another way of conceiving the stochastic process described by Equations (1) and (2) is as a tree of possible state sequences (Figure IV-4).

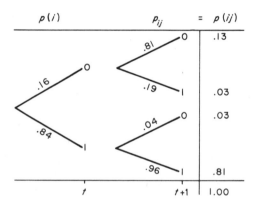

FIGURE IV-4. A tree diagram of the state and conditional probabilities of Equations (1) and (2). $p(ij)$ equals the product of $p(i)$ and p_{ij}.

The time axis shows the two state possibilities at time t and the two at time $t+1$ depending upon the choice at t. The initial branching portrays the stationary distribution of matrix P which is the absolute probability $p(i)$ of starting in state i. The branches between t and $t+1$ will be recognized as the elements p_{ij} of Equation (2), and sum to 1.0 for each starting state i. The column on the right gives the absolute probability of a particular state transition, each of which can now be visualized as a unique path through the tree. This absolute probability $p(ij)$ is the product of the state probability $p(i)$ of the initial branch and the transition probability p_{ij} of the second branch, as given in Equation (5). The absolute probabilities of all possible paths must, of course, sum to unity as in Equation (4). The tree diagram (Figure IV-4), state diagram (Figure IV-3), and matrix P [Equation (2)] are completely equivalent representations of this stochastic process.

Up to now it has been carefully noted that P is a one-step transition matrix, which means that state i and state j occur in adjacent time units. This can be illustrated by the following diagram.

State Sequence	=	0	1	0	0	1	1
1st transition (0 to 1)		$i \longrightarrow j$					
2nd transition (1 to 0)			$i \longrightarrow j$				
3rd transition (0 to 0)				$i \longrightarrow j$			
4th transition (0 to 1)					$i \longrightarrow j$		
5th transition (1 to 1)						$i \longrightarrow j$	
etc.							

In each transition ($\longrightarrow$), state j follows state i in the next time unit, i.e., at $t + 1$. The terminating state j for each transition is the beginning state i of the next. A two-step transition is one in which state i is separated from state j by two time units. This is illustrated as follows:

State Sequence	=	0	1	0	0	1	1
1st transition (0 to 0)		$i \longrightarrow j$					
2nd transition (1 to 0)			$i \longrightarrow j$				
3rd transition (0 to 1)				$i \longrightarrow j$			
4th transition (0 to 1)					$i \longrightarrow j$		
etc.							

Observe that the state at time unit $t+1$ is ignored although the starting state of each transition still advances by single steps. In the two-step matrix describing such transitions, the rows still correspond to the state at time t, but the columns now correspond to the state at time $t+2$, and the elements to the column state j at $t+2$ given row state i at t. It follows that an n-step matrix is one in which transitions from state i at time t to state j at time $t+n$ are tallied.[2] We now extend our notation as follows:

$P^{(1)}$ = one-step transition matrix with elements $p_{ij}^{(1)}$
$P^{(2)}$ = two-step transition matrix with elements $p_{ij}^{(2)}$
$P^{(n)}$ = n-step transition matrix with elements $p_{ij}^{(n)}$
$p_{ij}^{(n)}$ = probability of being in state j at time $t+n$ given that the process is in state i at time t

When the superscript (n) is omitted, assume that $n = 1$. We shall have recourse to this information later.

All the possible transitions in matrix $P^{(1)}$ occur in the raw data of monologue. Silence can continue as silence or give way to sound and, similarly, sound can continue or give way to silence. Such a transition matrix in which all transitions occur has an interesting property; its successive powers in general converge to a matrix P^* in which all columns are constant and each row sums to unity. As an illustration, the following are selections from the successive powers $[P^{(1)}]^n$ of the sample first-order matrix in Equation (2).

$$P^{(1)} = \begin{bmatrix} .81 & .19 \\ .04 & .96 \end{bmatrix} \qquad [P^{(1)}]^{14} = \begin{bmatrix} .18 & .82 \\ .15 & .85 \end{bmatrix}$$

$$[P^{(1)}]^2 = \begin{bmatrix} .66 & .34 \\ .06 & .94 \end{bmatrix} \qquad [P^{(1)}]^{18} = \begin{bmatrix} .16 & .84 \\ .15 & .85 \end{bmatrix}$$

$$[P^{(1)}]^6 = \begin{bmatrix} .33 & .67 \\ .12 & .88 \end{bmatrix} \qquad [P^{(1)}]^{26} = \begin{bmatrix} .16 & .84 \\ .16 & .84 \end{bmatrix}$$

$$[P^{(1)}]^{10} = \begin{bmatrix} .22 & .78 \\ .14 & .86 \end{bmatrix} \qquad [P^{(1)}]^{27} = \begin{bmatrix} .16 & .84 \\ .16 & .84 \end{bmatrix}$$

---

[2] Computed for a series of k consecutive states, a two-step matrix will have one less transition than a one-step matrix, i.e., $k-2$ instead of $k-1$ transitions, since the first two states will never be counted as outcomes. An n-step matrix will, therefore, have $k-n$ transitions. This shrinkage in frequencies is always insignificant in our data since $k \geqslant 1000$ and $n \leqslant 6$.

The last multiplication by $P^{(1)}$ yielding $[P^{(1)}]^{27}$ shows no change from power 26. It is apparent that as n gets very large the changes in the matrix become vanishingly small. The convergence here is complete to within the accuracy employed by power 26. However, if we carried a sufficiently large number of decimal places, the exponent for convergence could be arbitrarily large.[3] In symbols,

$$\lim_{n \to \infty} [P^{(1)}]^{n+1} = P^*$$ (7)

On convergence, in general, each row of P^* is its vector of absolute probabilities (marginals) which is also the *stationary distribution* of $P^{(1)}$, which means that the conditional probability of reaching a given state at $t+1$ is the same, regardless of the state occupied at time t. Thus, for the sample matrix in Equation (2), which may now be called $P^{(1)}$,

$$P^* = \begin{bmatrix} .16 & .84 \\ .16 & .84 \end{bmatrix}$$ (8)

each row being identical to V', which is the vector of state probabilities in Equation (1). Now, multiplying P^* by $P^{(1)}$, we see that P^* is carried into itself.

$$\begin{bmatrix} .16 & .84 \\ .16 & .84 \end{bmatrix} \begin{bmatrix} .81 & .19 \\ .04 & .96 \end{bmatrix} = \begin{bmatrix} .16 & .84 \\ .16 & .84 \end{bmatrix}$$

In other words, multiplication of the stationary distribution of a stochastic matrix by that matrix reproduces the stationary distribution.

---

[3] Obviously, since convergence is approached asymptotically, some criterion must be adopted for practical purposes. Originally, we adopted a commonsense but arbitrary criterion (Jaffe, Cassotta, & Feldstein, 1964). In subsequent work (Jaffe, Breskin, & Gerstman, 1969) a chi-square criterion of convergence was employed, which declared the stationary vector to have been reached when the power of the matrix did not differ significantly from the matrix predicted by the stationary distribution. This resulted in estimates of convergence at lower powers than were previously reported.

An examination of the tree of Figure IV-4 makes this result less mysterious. We see that the initial branching gives the state probabilities $p(i)$ which is the stationary distribution V' of Equation (1). The second branching gives the transition probabilities, elements p_{ij} of the stochastic matrix $P^{(1)}$. The column on the right gives the absolute probability, $p(ij)$, of each of the four paths through the tree, and these must sum to unity. Two of these paths result in a 0 outcome at $t+1$, i.e., transitions 0–0 and 1–0. The absolute probability of the first path, according to Equation (5), is

$$p(0)p_{00} = p(00) = .13$$

and of the second path is

$$p(1)p_{10} = p(10) = .03$$

The absolute probability of getting a zero, $p(0)$, is then the sum of the probabilities of the ways in which it can occur, i.e.,

$$p(0)p_{00} + p(1)p_{10} = p(0) = .16 \tag{9}$$

The remaining two paths through the tree result in a one at $t+1$. The absolute probability of the first is, similarly,

$$p(0)p_{01} = p(01) = .03$$

and of the second is

$$p(1)p_{11} = p(11) = .81$$

The absolute probability of getting a 1, $p(1)$, is therefore

$$p(0)p_{01} + p(1)p_{11} = p(1) = .84 \tag{10}$$

Equations (9) and (10), taken together, generate the stationary distribution

$$V' = [p(0), p(1)] = [.16, .84]$$

and they may be summarized in matrix notation as the single equation

$$[p(0), \ p(1)] \begin{bmatrix} p_{00} & p_{01} \\ p_{10} & p_{11} \end{bmatrix} = [p(0), \ p(1)]$$

which is the same as $V'P^{(1)} = V'$.

Finally, it is apparent that each row of the converged matrix P^* of Equation (8) is simply a repetition of the stationary distribution V' of Equation (1). Both P^* and V' are carried into themselves when multiplied by $P^{(1)}$.

Thus far we have described the kind of raw data—the zeros and ones—that our instrument extracts from an ongoing monologue, and a method for arranging the data, i.e., the stochastic matrices. The following section will show that such a method of data reduction leads to a model which accounts for the time patterns of vocal behavior in a monologue.

A. A ZERO-ORDER MARKOV MODEL FOR MONOLOGUE

The simplest stochastic model of the state sequence would be a zero-order Markov chain.[4] The model assumes statistical independence between the states of successive time units.

The transition matrix for such a process would have constant columns, each equal to the respective state probability, i.e., $p_{00} = p_{10} = p(0)$ and $p_{01} = p_{11} = p(1)$. Another way of saying this is that there is no sequential constraint in the state sequence; each state sampled could not be predicted better than by its absolute probability, even when given knowledge of the previous state; that is, $p_{ij} = p(j)$. The model assumes that the raw data of monologue yield a first-order stochastic matrix which is already converged; in our example, matrix P^* in Equation (7). Simple inspection

---

[4]A finite Markov chain is "a stochastic process which moves through a finite number of states, and for which the probability of entering a certain state depends only on the last state occupied" (From *Finite Markov Chains* by John G. Kemeny & J. Laurie Snell, copyright (©) 1960 by Litton Educational Publishing, Inc., by permission of van Nostrand Reinhold Company.) In our discussion this one-step dependency will be referred to as "first order." If the probability of entering a state depends only on the last *two* states occupied we refer to the model as "second order." Within this framework the lack of sequential dependency, the usual notion of statistical independence, is "zero order."

suffices to reject this model if we compare Equation (8) to Equation (2). The main diagonal elements of transition matrices for actual monologue are, at the sampling rate of 200 times per minute, always larger than the off-diagonal elements. The following is a typical matrix for monologue which represents the mean of 25 five-minute discourses.

$$P = \begin{bmatrix} .80 & .20 \\ .11 & .89 \end{bmatrix}$$

It is apparent that when somebody is either speaking or pausing, he is very likely to be in the same state 300 milliseconds later. Of course, a pause for breath, emphasis, or thinking has some minimum duration, as does even a brief interjection. Since these minimum durations are longer than 300 milliseconds (Appendix A), we find that immediately successive samples are very likely to encounter the same state.

B. A FIRST-ORDER MARKOV MODEL FOR MONOLOGUE

The transition matrices derived from the state sequences of monologue at this sampling rate thus suggest that prior events in the sequence exert some degree of constraint upon subsequent ones. A first-order Markov chain was, therefore, adopted as the simplest model of dependent probabilities for examination of these sequences. A first-order Markov chain is a stochastic process in which the future state of the process, given its present state, is independent of its past history, i.e., its state at time $t+1$, given its state at time t, is independent of its state at times $t-1, t-2, \ldots$. Recall our prior discussion of higher order transition matrices. Their elements $p_{ij}^{(n)}$ give the probability of being in state j at time $t+n$, given that the process was in state i at time t. The implications of a first-order Markov chain can best be demonstrated by expanding the tree of Figure IV-4 to include such longer range transitions. Imagine a ten-minute monologue sampled at 200 times per minute, yielding a total sequence of 2000 states. A way of visualizing this is to imagine the tree of possibilities for a sequence of 2000 states as an extension of Figure IV-4. There are two (2^1)

possibilities for the first state when $t = 1$, four (2^2) possible sequences for the first two states when $t = 2$, eight (2^3) possible sequences for the first three states when $t = 3$, and 2^{2000} possible
sequences for the total string when $t = 2000$. One and only one of
the unique paths through this tree is the actual sequence for the ten-
minute monologue which was observed. However, all 2^{2000} sequences might have happened but did not. It is physically impossible to draw the complete tree, but Figure IV-5 carries the argument through the first three of the two thousand inquiries.

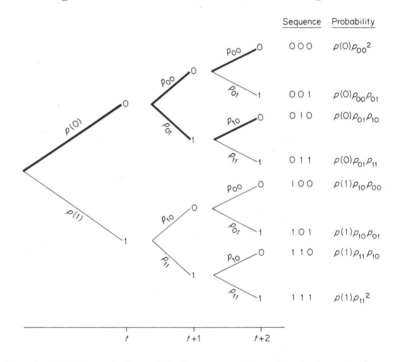

FIGURE IV-5. Tree of all possible sequences of sound and silence in three successive samples of a monologue. The paths shown in heavy lines are the two ways
of getting a 0 to 0 transition in two steps.

The tree in Figure IV-5 describes all possible sound–silence
sequences in three successive inquiries. For example, the sequence
1 0 1 describes a minimum pause of length 1 and the sequence 0 1 0
illustrates a minimum vocalization of length 1. The column on the

right gives the absolute probability of each particular sequence, i.e., of one unique path through the tree. In N samples there would be 2^N possible unique paths, but only one of them the actual observed process. We wish to know the probability of getting any particular sequence of zeros and ones. The model states that each one-step transition is statistically independent of its immediately prior state. The probability of the joint occurrences of independent events is, of course, given by the product of their separate probabilities. Therefore, the probability that some particular sequence of events be generated by a first-order Markov chain is the product of the absolute probability $p(i)$ of the initial state and the 1999 separate transition probabilities p_{ij}. By an easy computation this probability can be shown to be greatest when p_{ij} is estimated as being the value of the respective element of transition matrix $P^{(1)}$ This estimate is accordingly the "maximum likelihood" estimate.

The path probability is shown for each unique path in Figure IV-5 up to time $t+2$. For predictions of longer silence sequences, additional 0 to 0 transitions must be included in the equation for the probability of the given sequence. Additional 1 to 1 transitions will similarly predict longer vocalizations. The model assumes that the transition probabilities given by matrix P are stable (stationary) throughout the sequence. Thus, if the model is a good one, matrix P contains a complete description of the sequence and can predict the frequency of any special aspect that may be of psychological interest. This will be illustrated presently.

It can now be shown how the described tree measure for a first-order Markov chain predicts the longer range transition probabilities $p_{ij}^{(n)}$. Consider Figure IV-5 once again and ask what is the probability that the process be in state zero at $t+2$ if it is in state zero at t. This can occur via two different paths (heavy lines), i.e., 0 to 0 to 0, and 0 to 1 to 0. Thus, the probability of the event in question is the sum of the probabilities of the two ways it can occur. If Pr denotes the absolute probability of the sequence,

$$Pr\ (0\ 0\ 0) = p(0)p_{00}p_{00} = p(0)p_{00}^2$$
$$Pr\ (0\ 1\ 0) = p(0)p_{01}p_{10}$$

Adding the two equations gives the probability of the two-step event disregarding the *path* and considering only the state at t and $t+2$. State $i = 0$ or 1.

$$Pr\ (0\ i\ 0) = p(0)p_{00}{}^2 + p(0)p_{01}p_{10}$$
$$= p(0)[p_{00}{}^2 + p_{01}p_{10}]$$

Now consider only the bracketed expression $p_{00}{}^2 + p_{01}p_{10}$. Multiplying the first order P matrix by itself,

$$[P^{(1)}]^2 = \begin{bmatrix} p_{00} & p_{01} \\ p_{10} & p_{11} \end{bmatrix} \begin{bmatrix} p_{00} & p_{01} \\ p_{10} & p_{11} \end{bmatrix} = \begin{bmatrix} p_{00}{}^2 + p_{01}p_{10} & p_{00}p_{01} + p_{01}p_{11} \\ p_{10}p_{00} + p_{11}p_{10} & p_{10}p_{01} + p_{11}{}^2 \end{bmatrix}$$

it is seen that the conditional probability of a 0 to 0 transition in the squared matrix [when appropriately weighted by the probability $p(0)$ of the starting state] is precisely the expression derived from Figure IV-5 for a two-step transition. It can similarly be shown that all the other two-step transition probabilities derived from the tree, independent of path, are predicted by this squared matrix. In summary, the first-order Markov chain prediction for the matrix of two-step transition probabilities $P^{(2)}$ with elements $p_{ij}^{(2)}$ is

$$P^{(2)} = [P^{(1)}]^2$$

By an extension of this argument to a tree of three steps, it is easily shown that

$$P^{(3)} = [P^{(1)}]^3$$

is a necessary consequence of the first-order Markov chain model, and in general that

$$P^{(n)} = [P^{(1)}]^n$$

This consequence permits one test of the adequacy of the model. The n-step transition matrices $P^{(n)}$ may actually be computed from the raw data sequence and compared to the corresponding powers of the one-step P matrix. The actually observed elements $p_{ij}^{(n)}$ should not differ significantly from the values predicted by matrix multiplication of P with itself. This comparison is shown up to a power of 6 in Table IV-1.

TABLE IV-1

COMPARISONS OF OBTAINED AND PREDICTED MEAN CELL FREQUENCIES
OF HIGHER ORDER TRANSITION MATRICES AND THE
ROOT MEAN SQUARES (RMS) OF THEIR DIFFERENCES[a]

Obtained		Predicted		RMS	Power
420	72	—	—	—	1
72	438	—	—	—	1
365	127	371	121	7.39	2
126	384	121	389	7.27	2
325	167	337	155	14.86	3
166	344	155	356	14.66	3
300	192	314	178	18.47	4
191	319	178	332	18.26	4
285	207	297	195	18.40	5
206	304	194	316	18.19	5
277	215	286	206	15.38	6
214	297	206	305	14.91	6

[a] The powers refer to the predicted matrices. The table is taken from Jaffe, Cassotta, and Feldstein (1964) © 1964 by the American Association for the Advancement of Science.

There is an interesting relation between the superscript of an n-step matrix and the sampling rate r, such that r/n is another sampling rate at which the one-step matrix $P^{(1)}$ approximately equals $P^{(n)}$. Thus, $P^{(4)}$ based upon a rate of 200 inquiries per minute, will closely resemble $P^{(1)}$ based upon 50 inquiries per minute. The powers of $P^{(1)}$ may, therefore, be used to estimate the sampling rate below which sequential constraints between successive inquiries would no longer be detectable. This rate would be calculated from the power at which the matrix has satisfied a criterion of convergence, i.e., at which the states t and $t+1$ will be found to be statistically independent. For the monologue data in Table IV-1, the longest sampling interval for which constraints are still operative is roughly 2.1–2.7 seconds (see footnote 3). Sampling at greater intervals than this yields a transition matrix which looks as if it were derived from a zero-order Markov chain.

C. PREDICTING HISTOGRAMS OF PAUSE AND VOCALIZATION DURATIONS FOR MONOLOGUE

If we assume that this test of the fit of the model is adequate, as it seems to be on inspection, certain other consequences must follow which lead to specific predictions. It will be recalled from Chapter II that a "pause" is defined, by its boundary conditions, as a mutual silence which begins and ends with unilateral vocalization. Conversely, a unilateral vocalization is defined as a sound which begins and ends with mutual silence.

If Pr denotes the absolute probability of the event in question,

$$Pr \text{ (pause length 1)} = Pr \text{ (101)} \quad = p \text{ (1)} \, p_{10} p_{01}$$
$$Pr \text{ (pause length 2)} = Pr \text{ (1001)} \quad = p \text{ (1)} \, p_{10} p_{00} p_{01}$$
$$Pr \text{ (pause length 3)} = Pr \text{ (10001)} = p \text{ (1)} \, p_{10} p_{00}{}^2 p_{01}$$

in general,

$$Pr \text{ (pause length } L) = p \text{ (1)} \, p_{10} p_{00}{}^{L-1} p_{01} \tag{11}$$

similarly,

$$Pr \text{ (vocalization length } L) = p \text{ (0)} \, p_{01} p_{11}{}^{L-1} p_{10} \tag{12}$$

Equations (11) and (12) are the first-order Markov model predictions for the distributions of pause and vocalization durations, respectively. In both, L must be 1 or greater. If $L = 1$, then $p_{00}{}^{L-1}$ and $p_{11}{}^{L-1}$ are each 1, and the general expressions behave as if these transition probabilities were absent. Figures IV-6 and IV-7 show the pause and vocalization histograms presented previously in Chapter II, and the predictions of Equations (11) and (12). The probabilities all come from the first-order transition matrix $P^{(1)}$ and its stationary distribution.

The failure of the model for very long pauses is apparent, as is its adequacy for the overwhelming proportion of short pauses. The

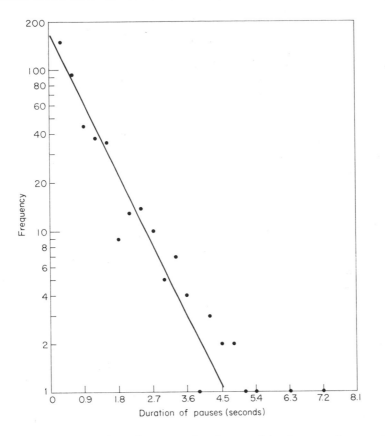

FIGURE IV-6. A typical log-frequency distribution of the duration of pauses that occur in a monologue. The straight line represents the predicted distribution based upon a first-order Markov chain. The distribution is derived from a monologue lasting 20 minutes.

former occur more frequently than would be expected by the linear prediction.

For present purposes, the Markovian prediction of time patterns of monologue is sufficiently developed to serve as an introduction to our analogous treatment of dialogue. As will be evident, a completely parallel argument follows naturally for a two-speaker system, although the ongoing process will have four states instead of two.

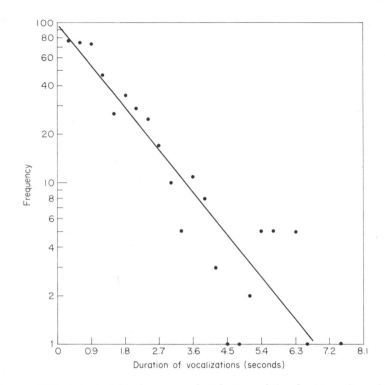

FIGURE IV-7. A typical log-frequency distribution of the duration of vocaliza-tions that occur in a monologue. The straight line represents the predicted distribu-tion based upon a first-order Markov chain. The distribution is derived from a mono-logue lasting 20 minutes.

II. Time Patterns of Dialogue

The extension of the two-state monologue model to dialogue is straightforward. The "voice keys" of separate speakers in conversa-tion are simultaneously sampled and the transition matrices $P_{ij}^{(\eta)}$ are computed as before but with i and j now equal to 0,1,2, and 3.[5] The

---

[5] The four states are named 0,1,2 and 3 rather than the more conventional 1,2,3 and 4 because the former corresponds to the binary notation describing the con-figuration of the two voice relays. (See legend Figure II-2.)

monologue states of the speakers combine to form four dyadic states, as follows:

Participant state			Dyadic state	
B	A			
0	0	=	0	= both silent
0	1	=	1	= A vocalizing
1	0	=	2	= B vocalizing
1	1	=	3	= simultaneous speech

The raw data for dialogue can thus be viewed as a sequence of the numbers 0,1,2, and 3, corresponding to the dyadic states as just defined. In this four-state process, the transition matrices $P^{(n)}$ with elements $p_{ij}^{(n)}$ give the conditional probabilities of reaching state j from state i in n steps (where $i,j = 0,1,2,3$).

$$P^{(n)} = \begin{bmatrix} p_{00}^{(n)} & p_{01}^{(n)} & p_{02}^{(n)} & p_{03}^{(n)} \\ p_{10}^{(n)} & p_{11}^{(n)} & p_{12}^{(n)} & p_{13}^{(n)} \\ p_{20}^{(n)} & p_{21}^{(n)} & p_{22}^{(n)} & p_{23}^{(n)} \\ p_{30}^{(n)} & p_{31}^{(n)} & p_{32}^{(n)} & p_{33}^{(n)} \end{bmatrix}$$

$P^{(n)}$ thus summarizes the time patterns of a dialogue and is obtained from the raw transition frequency matrix exactly as was described previously for monologue. It will now be apparent why the second paragraph of this chapter described monologue as a "special case" of dialogue. Note that if speaker B were completely silent, two rows and two columns of the matrix would consist of zeros (states 2 and 3), thereby reducing the model to a two-state (2 by 2) monologue matrix.[6]

The dialogue matrix is one in which all transitions are possible, so our earlier description of matrix convergence is appropriate here. The stationary distribution, V', of a dialogue matrix is the vector $[p(0), p(1), p(2), p(3)]$. As previously argued, were no constraints operating between the successive states of dialogue, we should

---

[6]The theoretical notion suggested is a definition of monologue as a dialogue with one silent participant.

expect the probabilities of each row of matrix $P^{(1)}$ to approximate this stationary distribution. Inspection of the transition probabilities derived from a typical 20-minute conversation below is sufficient to reject the assumption of sequential independence.

$$
P^{(1)} = \begin{bmatrix} .66 & .16 & .17 & .01 \\ .11 & .87 & .01 & .01 \\ .17 & .02 & .80 & .01 \\ .00 & .36 & .32 & .32 \end{bmatrix}
\qquad
\begin{array}{c} \text{Stationary} \\ \text{Distribution} \\ .29 \\ .39 \\ .31 \\ \underline{.01} \\ 1.00 \end{array}
$$

Thus, it must be presumed that sequential constraints are operative in dialogue as in monologue; it would be rather surprising if this were found not to be so.

A. SINGLE-SOURCE MODEL

It must be emphasized at this juncture that the sampled configuration of the two voice relays defines a unitary "dyadic state." No hypothesis as to how the separate sequential behaviors of the participants combine to produce the dyadic state sequence is offered. In the absence of such an interactive hypothesis, the model now to be considered is compatible with the notion of a single rather than a double speech source.

1. A First-Order Markov Model for Dialogue

We may now ask whether a first-order Markov chain is as tenable a model for this four-state process as it was for the two-state process of monologue. As before, it is required that

$$P^{(n)} = [P^{(1)}]^n$$

but now i and j each assumes the values 0,1,2, and 3. Table IV-2 compares $P^{(n)}$ (the obtained matrices) with $[P^{(1)}]^n$ (the predicted matrices) up to a power of 6.

TABLE IV-2

OBSERVED MEAN PROBABILITY AND FREQUENCY TRANSITION MATRICES
FROM FIRST THROUGH SIXTH ORDER AND PREDICTED MEAN
PROBABILITY MATRICES FROM SECOND THROUGH SIXTH POWER[a]

Observed								Predicted				Power
Probabilities				Frequencies				probabilities				
.732	.186	.079	.002	882	196	90	2	—	—	—	—	1
.147	.845	.004	.003	204	1305	7	4	—	—	—	—	
.169	.030	.787	.014	82	15	384	6	—	—	—	—	
.075	.260	.365	.301	1	5	7	7	—	—	—	—	
.563	.299	.132	.005	696	319	151	5	.580	.294	.122	.004	2
.240	.741	.015	.003	333	1159	23	6	.233	.743	.020	.004	
.282	.079	.625	.014	137	38	306	7	.263	.083	.638	.016	
.176	.271	.437	.116	3	6	9	3	.178	.310	.396	.116	
.465	.362	.167	.007	586	387	191	7	.493	.358	.144	.005	3
.290	.675	.032	.004	401	1068	46	6	.284	.674	.038	.004	
.363	.128	.497	.012	178	61	243	6	.315	.141	.530	.015	
.264	.290	.393	.054	5	6	8	1	.254	.328	.366	.052	
.418	.391	.184	.007	532	420	211	7	.442	.397	.155	.006	4
.310	.636	.050	.005	428	1014	71	7	.315	.625	.056	.005	
.413	.171	.406	.011	202	81	199	5	.343	.195	.448	.014	
.338	.311	.332	.020	6	7	7	1	.303	.343	.327	.027	
.399	.404	.190	.007	511	435	218	7	.412	.422	.160	.006	5
.314	.614	.067	.005	434	984	94	8	.333	.590	.073	.005	
.441	.204	.345	.010	217	97	169	5	.358	.243	.386	.012	
.333	.341	.315	.011	6	7	7	0	.333	.359	.292	.017	
.396	.410	.188	.006	507	441	216	7	.395	.438	.162	.006	6
.312	.600	.082	.006	431	965	115	9	.344	.564	.087	.005	
.450	.232	.309	.009	222	110	151	4	.366	.284	.338	.011	
.344	.361	.286	.010	6	8	6	0	.350	.375	.263	.013	

[a] Each 4 by 4 frequency matrix and each 4 by 4 probability matrix is the mean of 50 individual matrices, each of which was derived from a 16-minute stress-inducing dialogue. The table is taken from Jaffe, Feldstein, and Cassotta (1967a).

The comparisons are expressed as mean conditional probabilities. The mean frequencies on which the calculations are based are labeled the "observed frequency" matrices. The reason for including these is that certain transitions are extremely rare. The normalized matrix, with each row summing to unity, gives a distorted impression of the magnitude of error in such cases.

Inspection plus a chi-square test of the first- versus the second-order model predictions[7] indicate that the time pattern of dyadic vocal interaction is usefully described as a first-order Markov chain. However, the comparison of matrices by chi-square tests tells us little about the usefulness of the model for prediction of other phenomena of interest. Tests of other consequences of the model are the ultimate criteria of when a fit is "good enough." That is the next step.

2. Prediction of Pause, Switching Pause, and Vocalization Duration Histograms in Dialogue

Assuming that a first-order Markov chain fits the raw data of dialogue reasonably well, we may ask how much of the descriptive classification of the earlier chapters is derived from the first-order matrix under the assumptions of the model.

As in the case of monologue, equations may be written for these events as follows.[8]

$$Pr \text{ (pause length } L \text{ for speaker A)} = p(1)p_{10}p_{00}^{L-1}p_{01}$$
$$Pr \text{ (pause length } L \text{ for speaker B)} = p(2)p_{20}p_{00}^{L-1}p_{02}$$

$$Pr \text{ (switching pause length } L \text{ for speaker A)} = p(1)p_{10}p_{00}^{L-1}p_{02}$$
$$Pr \text{ (switching pause length } L \text{ for speaker B)} = p(2)p_{20}p_{00}^{L-1}p_{01}$$

---

[7]Chi-square tests of second versus first order processes were significant at the .05 level in 159 out of 200 16-minute dialogues. These were the 200 dialogues sampled in Table IV-2 and analyzed further in Table IV-3. This indicates that the process usually is at least second order, i.e., that the state at $t+1$ given the state at t is somewhat dependent upon the state at $t-1$. Nevertheless, estimates based on first order data were found to be adequate for present purposes, as will be shown subsequently. Presumably the second order dependence accounts for but a small portion of the variance relative to the first order dependency. The details of this test for the order of the Markov process are given in Anderson and Goodman (1957).

[8]A simplifying assumption, that state 3 does not occur, is made to shorten the equations. Actually a very small percentage of pauses and switching pauses depend upon transitions involving simultaneous speech. If state 3 is disregarded, there are only four possible combinations of boundary conditions, since unilateral vocalization by *either* speaker may initiate and/or terminate a mutual silence.

$$Pr \text{ (vocalization length } L \text{ for speaker A)} = p(0)p_{01}p_{11}^{L-1}p_{10}$$
$$Pr \text{ (vocalization length } L \text{ for speaker B)} = p(0)p_{02}p_{22}^{L-1}p_{20}$$

for $L \geqslant 1$. These predictions from the first-order P matrix are shown together with the exponential distributions of Chapter II in Figures IV-8, IV-9, and IV-10.

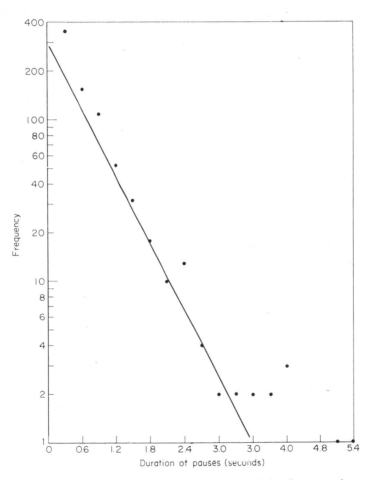

FIGURE IV-8. A typical log-frequency distribution of the duration of pauses of one speaker in a dialogue. The straight line represents the predicted distribution based upon a first-order Markov chain. The distribution is derived from a dialogue lasting 50 minutes.

A potentially serious shortcoming of the single-source model can now be demonstrated. It is first necessary to ponder the descriptive classification presented in Chapter II, for it is the exponential distribution of these events we are attempting to model. Recall that these events were defined by their boundary conditions which

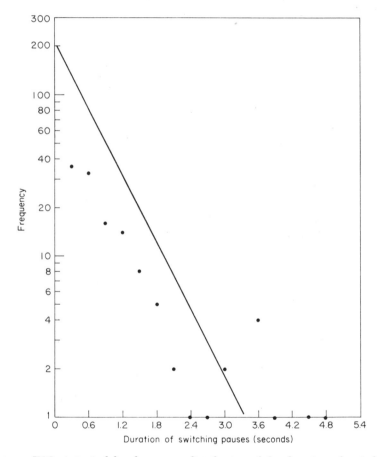

FIGURE IV-9. A typical log-frequency distribution of the duration of switching pauses of one speaker in a dialogue. The straight line represents the predicted distribution based upon a first-order Markov chain. The distribution is derived from a dialogue lasting 50 minutes.

allow us to infer the behavioral state of *both* speakers. For example, a pause on the part of either speaker allows us to infer that the other participant is in a "nonutterance," and presumably a "listening" mode, for he has remained silent throughout the pause. The switching pause allows us to infer that the speaker holding the floor has

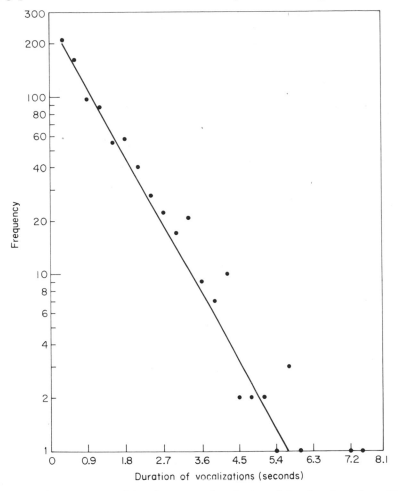

FIGURE IV-10. A typical log-frequency distribution of the duration of vocalizations of one speaker in a dialogue. The straight line represents the predicted distribution based upon a first-order Markov chain. The distribution is derived from a dialogue lasting 50 minutes.

entered the listening mode when the previous listener switches to the utterance mode. These are guesses, of course. The presumed listener may remain silent during a pause because he is asleep, distracted, or muttering a hostile retort under his breath. The reader can undoubtedly describe many other configurations of internal states that could manifest themselves as a joint silence. Nevertheless, reference to the boundaries of such symmetrical events permits a reasonable guess as to the probable states of the participants.

We are deprived of such guidelines by the Markovian model. Here a joint silence loses track of its starting state after one transition, which is the limit of the memory of a first-order Markov chain. All joint silences of two steps or more are, therefore, confounded. This precarious status of our single-source silence (state zero) will be resolved in Chapter V. For the moment, it should be clearly realized that the present predictions of the silence distributions cannot make such a discrimination, since they all depend upon the confounded transition from state zero to itself, i.e., p_{00}. Thus, the four exponential distributions of silence, two for pauses and two for switching pauses, must of mathematical necessity have identical means. This may be a serious limitation of the "single-source" Markovian model if it should turn out that the means of these silence distributions are empirically different. Examination of Figures IV-8 and IV-9 shows that switching pauses are less predictable than pauses. This may result from the lower frequencies of switching pauses and the related fact that p_{00} is mainly an index of prolongation of pauses.

The vocalization distributions as illustrated in Figure IV-10 are less confounded than are the silence distributions for the simple reason that vocalization is rarely mutual, the absolute probability of state 3 usually being less than .05. In contrast, state zero may occur an order of magnitude more frequently; .50 is not an unusual figure. Thus, vocalization is more subject to isolation as a relatively individual characteristic. The inference that the inactive participant is in a "listening" state during vocalization seems more warranted than during mutual silence. Mathematically, the predicted vocalization histograms above, based upon the separate transition probabilities p_{11} and p_{22}, may have very different means for the two speakers.

In summary, then, the problem of predicting silence histograms by means of a first-order single-source model lies in the confounded transition from state 0 to itself. A first-order process considers transitions of only one step. Thus, it loses track of the boundary conditions of dyadic silence greater than length 1. In other words it has a one-step memory and predicts longer sequences by juxtaposing the one-step transition probabilities. If the process remains in a state for more than one step, the model simply does not say how it arrived there. The model predicts identical means for the distributions of these four types of dyadic silence at durations greater than length 1. Although the relationship implied by this prediction may indeed occur empirically, there is no *a priori* necessity for its occurrence.[9] The vocalization histograms are not subject to this objection. Unilateral vocalization may show very different means for the two speakers in terms of a single-source model.

Finally, a Markov model is linear (as displayed on semilog coordinates) and predicts that events lasting longer than a certain duration become vanishingly improbable. However, the tails of the distributions in Figures IV-6 and IV-8 indicate that a greater number of long events occur than would be predicted by the model. The notion of a second exponential to account for the distribution of such excessively long events has been suggested for many years (Chapple, 1939). One hypothesis that might be made about these events is that a different psychological state obtains past the point at which the model begins to fail grossly, e.g., the "awkward silence."

3. Prediction of Speaker Switching

A parameter of a Markov chain which may be computed from the transition matrix is the mean waiting time in a set of states prior to the first occurrence of some other state. The theory of absorbing Markov chains is used (Kemeny & Snell, 1960).

Although transition from any of the four dyadic states to any other is in fact possible, one may arbitrarily assume that when a

---

[9] A second-order model, one with a memory of two previous steps, would encounter this limitation with silence sequences greater than length 2. An *n*th order model would be similarly limited with silence durations greater than length *n* (see also footnote 4, this chapter).

given state is entered it will never be left. To use a marketing analogy, consider the following[10]: Four soft-drink companies are competing for the market. All four drinks taste the same, but one of them contains a very compelling addictive drug. Thus, if a person drinks the drugged brand he will remain "loyal" and never again drink the others. We have four possible states: (1) drink brand A; (2) drink brand B; (3) drink brand C; and (4) drink brand D. Assume that B is drugged. Drinking it is an "absorbing" state, i.e., once entered it will never be left. The drinking of brand A, C, or D is a "nonabsorbing" state, for the drinker may later change to any other brand. Suppose people are chosen at random and the brand being drunk is noted at successive times — say, every week. We might be interested in the average number of time periods it takes for a person who starts with a nonabsorbing brand to try the drugged one. If the process is Markovian, we can compute the average number of time periods it takes for the process starting in a nonabsorbing state to reach the specified absorbing state.

We may similarly investigate our own four-state process, each time unit defining a state. The utterance domain for speaker A is composed of a sequence of states 0 and 1 and 3, terminated by a switch to state 2. Similarly, the utterance domain for speaker B consists of a sequence of states 0 and 2 and 3 terminated by state 1. If we make state 2 absorbing and begin in state 1, then the mean number of steps in states 0, 1, and 3 before encountering state 2 would be a rough estimate of mean utterance length of speaker A. Making state 1 absorbing permits the same calculation for speaker B. The sum of the two means is the average length of the cycle from the beginning of one speaker's utterance until the beginning of his next utterance. Dividing the total time of the interaction by the average cycle length estimates the number of switches. Product–moment and intraclass correlations may then be computed between frequency of switches estimated on the basis of Markov chain theory and actual counts thereof. These correlations were computed for the 200 sixteen-minute experimental interviews sampled in Table IV-2 and are summarized in Table IV-3. The experiment is the first study outlined in Chapter III.

---

[10] We thank Mr. Peter Trenholme of the Department of Mathematical Statistics, Columbia University, for this charming psychopharmacological imagery regarding "absorbing states."

TABLE IV-3
CORRELATIONS BETWEEN ACTUAL AND ESTIMATED
FREQUENCY OF SWITCHES

Interview[a]	I	II	III	IV
Product–moment correlation	.93	.96	.91	.90
Intraclass correlation	.90	.89	.87	.84

[a] For each interview $N = 50$.

The high correlations further support the appropriateness of a first order model. That is to say, if we assume the time patterns of these dialogues to have been produced by a four-state Markov process, and the observed transition matrix to be the maximum likelihood matrix for that process, we would be able to account for the distribution of another class of commonsense long range events in dialogue. These events (speaker switches) occur on the average at 3–10 second intervals in these dialogues, whereas the sequential constraints measured are between samples 300 milliseconds apart. The implication is that such short range sequential probabilities are approximately stationary, or stable, over the 16 minutes of the dialogue.

4. Prediction of Time Sharing

A derived index, the estimated time sharing ratio, is defined as the larger of the two estimated mean durations of utterances divided by their sum. Therefore, when the time is shared equally, the ratio

TABLE IV-4
CORRELATIONS OF OBTAINED AND ESTIMATED
TIME SHARING RATIOS

Interview[a]	I	II	III	IV
Product–moment correlation	.95	.96	.98	.96
Intraclass correlation	.91	.95	.98	.94

[a] For each interview $N = 50$.

approaches a minimum value of .5, whereas if one speaker monopolizes all the available time, the ratio approaches its maximum value of 1.0. Pearson product–moment correlations and intraclass correlations were obtained for time sharing ratios between actual data and the estimates obtained from the first order transition matrix (Table IV-4).

The magnitudes of the correlations are similar to those found for the estimates of frequency of speaker switches.

5. Limitations of the Single-Source Model

The interaction assumption of the single-source model is that the vocal behavior of each participant is so entirely *dependent* upon that of the other than no statement regarding the rules of combination is necessary. This is tantamount to saying that the obtained 4 by 4 matrix was produced by a "dyadic state generator," rather than two separate individuals.[11] In spite of this admittedly uncomfortable assumption, several important interactive phenomena and a few "individual" ones could nevertheless be accounted for.

Perhaps a greater handicap is that the single-source model requires 12 parameters (three elements of each row of the P matrix define the fourth) in order to predict 16 matrix elements. In other words, the matrix has 12 degrees of freedom. This is not terribly parsimonious.

The most important drawback of the single-source model is that the "dyadic" parameters cannot be assigned to the separate participants in order to predict their future interactions with others. It is desirable that a behavioral model account not only for the context in which the behavior is observed, but also predict new instances thereof. From this point of view, the single-source dialogue matrix can be used for prediction in only two ways: (a) by being considered the best estimate of matrices derived from future dialogues of the same two participants; and (b) by its use as a "normative model" which permits the prediction of dialogue matrices from other participants under similar conditions.

---

[11]This maneuver amounts to an arbitrary definition of the dyad as the minimal unit of social interaction which need not be further subdivided. Theoretical implications of this assumption are discussed in Chapter VI.

To roughly examine the effect of the "normative" assumption, the mean of a randomly selected set of ten P matrices was computed and designated the "normative model." This mean matrix was then compared to each of another set of ten randomly selected matrices obtained under the same controlled conditions as was the first set.

6. Tests of "Goodness of Fit"

Before assessing the fit of the "normative" and other models, a word is in order regarding our approach to this assessment. Our matrices comprise thousands of observations (up to 60 minutes of dialogue at 200 samples/minute). The power of conventional tests to find a statistically significant difference between any given model and the observed matrix is, therefore, very great. However, statistical tests cannot tell us whether the significant difference is indeed meaningful in the context of our intended purpose. They can tell us, however, which of *two* proposed models yields a better description of the observed data.

Edwards (1965) has summarized the matter as follows:

> A man from Mars, asked whether or not your suit fits you, would have trouble answering. He could notice the discrepancies between its measurements and yours, and might answer no; he could notice that you did not trip over it, and might answer yes. But give him two suits and ask him which fits you better, and his task starts to make sense, though it still has its difficulties . . . no procedure can test the goodness of fit of a single model to data in any satisfactory way. But procedures for comparing the goodness of fit of two or more models to the same data are easy to come by, entirely appropriate, . . .

Each of our models is expressed as a transition matrix. Under the Markovian assumption, each matrix defines a stochastic process which is a sequence of dyadic states; and each matrix embodies an estimate of the probability or likelihood of the total behavioral sequence described. For the four-state process it can be shown that this estimate is greatest when generated by the observed P matrix (the single-source model). The likelihood of the sequence may similarly be estimated for some less general four-state model, e.g., one in which some special restriction has been hypothesized. If the probability were as great as the single-source model, the likelihood ratio of the two estimates would be unity. Otherwise the Neyman-Pearson statistic (see Appendix C), which is distributed as chi-square, constitutes a single discrepancy score and a rough indication of "goodness of fit." This permits a ranking of the hypotheses in terms of their closeness to the observed data (Jaffe, 1968). The statistic itself is treated as a score, or distance measure, rather than as a test of significance for reasons discussed above. That is, for a chi-square with very large N, the probability that even a very small percentage difference would be found to be significant would approach unity. As a dependent variable, however, the Neyman-Pearson statistic can be used in conventional analyses of variance to test certain predictions of the model in conversational experiments.

Other assessments of fit consist of tests of mathematical consequences of the model such as the mean and distribution of the categories of the descriptive classification. So we have two tests of goodness of fit: (a) comparison of Neyman-Pearson statistics for competing models against the single-source (maximum likelihood) model; (b) comparison of predictions which are mathematical consequences of the competing models.

Returning to our assessment of the normative model, the Neyman-Pearson statistic was computed for each of the ten randomly selected P matrices against the normative model. The values ranged from 258.5 to 767.6, all highly significant differences, with a mean of 398.5. This may be thought of as a baseline against which to assess the adequacy of the separate source model presented in the next section.

B.   SEPARATE SOURCE MODEL

The preceding description of dialogic time patterns as a Markov chain neglected the fact that the process was derived from two separate speech sources. To do so requires at least one additional assumption about the influence of the speakers on each other, i.e., the rules of temporal interaction. This is the task of the present section.

The initial attempt to model the rules of temporal interaction was by Jaffe and Norman (1964). They posed the problem of decomposing the dyadic system into the separate monologues of the participants such that the dialogue rhythm could again be concatenated

by means of an interactive hypothesis. They approached the con-
catenation problem with four basic assumptions:

(1) The participants make *independent* decisions to vocalize at
any time t, each with some fixed probability which is characteristic
of the individual speaker.

(2) These independent decisions are contingent upon *both* their
own behavior *and* that of the other participant at time $t-1$.

(3) Both speakers use identical decision rules such that only one
holds the floor at a time.

(4) An unobserved Markov chain underlies the four overt states
of the dialogic temporal pattern.

The model as originally proposed was intractable mathematically.
Maximum likelihood estimates of the parameters were unobtainable, so the model was simulated instead. It was subsequently sup-
planted by the "independent decision" model described in the
following paragraph which retains, with certain qualifications, the
first three assumptions. The fourth assumption is revived in
Chapter V and in Jaffe (1967).

As the basis for a reasonable hypothesis to account for dyadic
states in terms of the interaction of separate speakers, we shall
draw upon a commonsense observation which is bolstered by considerable experimental evidence. It is that speaking and listening
are incompatible; or stated differently, a person is unlikely to be in
both a speaking and listening state at the same instant. Perhaps
"some critical component of the speech apparatus must be actively
involved in the process of understanding speech" (Miller, 1963).
Perhaps simultaneous encoding and decoding of speech exceeds
the information processing ability of the brain. Whatever the neurophysiological reason, these two states, i.e., speaking and listening,
tend to alternate in time. We, therefore, have some basis for the
assumption that at the very moment of vocalizing, a speaker is
relatively inattentive to his listener. That is to say, he acts, or fails
to act, momentarily independently of the other. An additional
assumption is that he is nevertheless aware both of his own *and*
the other person's behavior of the previous 300 millisecond instant,
which is well within the range of short-term memory. Taking these
together, we assume that a speaker has a probability of speaking
at any time $t+1$ which is conditional upon the dyadic state at time

t, but which is independent of the other participant at the instant of execution.[12] In other words, the participants make *independent decisions* to speak or remain silent at any time $t+1$ with probabilities conditional upon their joint history at time t. This "independent decision model"[13] is a completely general eight parameter model (four parameters per speaker). It meets some of the objections raised to the single-source model in the previous section, since: (a) it is more parsimonious than the single-source model, having eight parameters instead of 12; (b) it accounts for the P matrix of the "single-source" model in terms of the interaction of separate speakers; and (c) it provides estimates of "individual parameters" which can be used to predict future interactions with either the same or another speaker.

As a model which generates a first order Markov process, the hypothesized independent decision rule also operates within the confines of a single transition, i.e., within 300 milliseconds. It is derived as follows:

Let

$$q_i = \text{probability that A speaks at } t+1 \text{ given dyadic state } i \text{ at } t$$
$$r_i = \text{probability that B speaks at } t+1 \text{ given dyadic state } i \text{ at } t$$
$$1-q_i = \text{probability that A is silent at } t+1 \text{ given dyadic state } i \text{ at } t$$
$$1-r_i = \text{probability that B is silent at } t+1 \text{ given dyadic state } i \text{ at } t$$

---

[12]A somewhat different formulation is proposed by Jaffe (1968). "This model implicitly embodies an assumption about the possibility of participant–observation, that is, the ability of an individual to process incoming information at the instant he is deciding to act and doing so. Participation is defined as a current *personal* decision to vocalize or not; observation as the short-term memory of a concluded *interpersonal* event. The model asserts that the personal decision to act is constrained *only* by the interpersonal configuration of the immediate past, which implies that an individual observes the outcome of previous interactions but ceases to observe at the moment of participation. A Markov chain can be generated from these assumptions" (p. 265).

[13]This descendant of the Jaffe and Norman (1964) model was suggested by Prof. Alex Heller, Department of Mathematics, Graduate Center, City University of New York, who was a consultant on the project. See also Jaffe, Feldstein, and Cassotta (1967b).

where $(i = 0,1,2,3)$ exactly as in the single-source model. The maximum likelihood estimates for these eight parameters, q_0, q_1, q_2, q_3 and r_0, r_1, r_2, r_3, are

$$q_i = p_{i1} + p_{i3} \qquad (13)$$

$$r_i = p_{i2} + p_{i3} \qquad (14)$$

The probabilities on the right side of Equations (13) and (14) are the transition probabilities from the P matrix of the single-source model.

As an illustration, the probability that A decides (independently) to talk at $t+1$, given mutual silence (state 0) at t, is q_0, and

$$q_0 = p_{01} + p_{03}$$

That is, p_{01} is the probability that A terminates the mutual silence alone, whereas p_{03} is also the probability that he terminates the silence, but just when B has made the same decision. Similarly, the probability of an independent decision to talk by B, given a preceding state of mutual silence, is r_0, and

$$r_0 = p_{02} + p_{03}$$

That is, p_{02} is the probability that B terminates the mutual silence alone, whereas p_{03} is also the probability that he terminates the silence, but just when A has made the same decision.

The parameter estimates thus translate the logical assumptions of the model as stated above. Having now defined the independent probability of each speaker talking at $t+1$ given that the preceding *dyadic* state was 0, the probability of a joint event, i.e., that *both* speakers begin at $t+1$, given mutual silence at t, is just the product of their separate chances of doing so; in symbols, $q_0 r_0$. This would yield a 0 to 3 transition in terms of dyadic states. By the same argument, the probability that both remain silent at $t+1$ given mutual silence at t is the product of their separate probabilities of not speaking; in symbols, $(1-q_0)(1-r_0)$, yielding a 0 to 0 transition. The probability that A remains silent while B starts in the same situation is $(1-q_0)r_0$, yielding a 0 to 2 dyadic state transition, and so forth.

In this manner, all 16 possible transitions may be generated in terms of the independent decisions, yielding a new matrix $\tilde{P}$, which summarizes the predicted transition probabilities.

$$\tilde{P} = \begin{bmatrix} (1-q_0)(1-r_0) & q_0(1-r_0) & (1-q_0)r_0 & q_0r_0 \\ (1-q_1)(1-r_1) & q_1(1-r_1) & (1-q_1)r_1 & q_1r_1 \\ (1-q_2)(1-r_2) & q_2(1-r_2) & (1-q_2)r_2 & q_2r_2 \\ (1-q_3)(1-r_3) & q_3(1-r_3) & (1-q_3)r_3 & q_3r_3 \end{bmatrix} \quad (15)$$

One test of the goodness of fit of this model would be to derive the $\tilde{P}$ matrix for each of the randomly selected dialogues which were used in the previous section to test the single-source against the normative model. It will be recalled that a Neyman-Pearson statistic was calculated to compare a mean, or normative matrix and each of ten randomly selected matrices. The statistic in individual comparisons ranged from 258.5 to 767.6 with a mean of 398.5. In the present comparison, the statistic was calculated for the independent decision $\tilde{P}$ matrices of the same ten cases and ranged between 35.0 and 157.5 with a mean of 94.2 (Table IV-5). Thus, for a given case the independent decision model matrix resembles that for the single-source model more closely than does a normative matrix derived from other comparable dialogues.

Another test of the adequacy of the independent decision model would be to derive certain necessary mathematical consequences which show how well it accounts for certain gross phenomena of the dialogue, such as speaker switching. Recall that in the previous section the single-source model accounted for this phenonenon remarkably well, correlations being in the .90s. By comparison, the product moment correlation of observed frequencies of speaker switching in 60 sixteen-minute dialogues with the frequencies estimated from the respective $\tilde{P}$ matrices was .80. Apparently the independent decision hypothesis regarding the interaction of speakers accounts for this aspect of dyadic behavior about as well as does the single-source model. To the extent that it fits the data less adequately, the assumptions of the independent decision model require examination. One approach is to examine the pattern of the discrepancy for some systematic deviation. This may be illustrated by simple inspection of the average stationary distribution of state probabilities which was predicted by the independent decision model for 16 randomly selected dialogues (Table IV-6). It is apparent that states 0 and 3 are overestimated and states 1 and 2

TABLE IV-5

NEYMAN-PEARSON STATISTICS COMPARING
EACH OF 10 RANDOMLY SELECTED
DIALOGUES[a] WITH THEIR RESPECTIVE
INDEPENDENT DECISION MATRICES AND
WITH A NORMATIVE MATRIX

Independent decision model	Normative model
115.2	393.1
101.5	264.7
157.5	326.5
132.0	308.9
74.7	767.6
80.5	258.5
74.4	529.0
105.6	295.5
35.0	464.7
65.5	376.5
Mean	
94.2	398.5
SD	
33.7	148.2

[a]Duration of each dialogue was 20 minutes.

TABLE IV-6

DISCREPANCY PATTERN OF MEAN STATIONARY DISTRIBUTION
$(N = 16)$

State	Single–source model		Independent decision model
0	.169	<	.208
1	.397	>	.351
2	.394	>	.368
3	.040	<	.073

underestimated. A conceivable explanation for this pattern of discrepancy follows.

In Figure IV-11a, known as a Venn diagram, assume that the en-

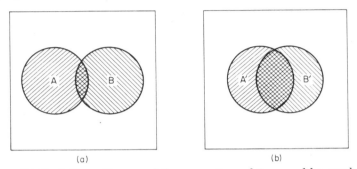

(a)   (b)

FIGURE IV-11. A Venn diagram of the proportions of time used by speakers A, B, A', and B' for speech (areas within the circles) and silence (area within the rectangles but outside the circles). The overlapping areas of (a) A, B and (b) A', B' represent proportions of time used for simultaneous speech.

closing rectangle has area 1 and represents the total speaking time available during the course of a dialogue. The area of the shaded circle marked A represents the proportion of the time (or probability) that speaker A vocalizes. The area of the shaded circle marked B represents the proportion of the time utilized by speaker B. The area of the intersection of the circles, doubly crosshatched, is the proportion of the time that A and B would speak simultaneously if they interacted randomly, i.e., as if they were unaware of the other's presence. The total shaded area is the proportion of the time in which some vocalization occurred. The white area within the rectangle but outside the shaded area represents the proportion of the time that both participants would be silent. Note that for *fixed proportions* of A and B, respectively, the area of intersection (simultaneous speech) and the area of mutual silence must vary concomitantly. The greater the overlap, the greater the area outside the circles. Expressing this in terms of sets, consider the dialogues represented by Figure IV-11a,b.

Let

$$p(A) = p(A') = \text{probability that first speaker talks}$$
$$p(B) = p(B') = \text{probability that second speaker talks}$$

Since

$$p(A \cup B) + p(A \cap B) = p(A) + p(B)$$

and

$$p(A' \cup B') + p(A' \cap B') = p(A') + p(B')$$

then

$$p(A \cap B) < p(A' \cap B') \Rightarrow p(A \cup B) > p(A' \cup B')$$
$$\Rightarrow 1 - p(A \cup B) < 1 - p(A' \cup B')$$

We are led to the conclusion that interacting speakers are not quite as independent as this separate source model assumes. The model nevertheless is useful as is shown in the section which follows.

III.   A Predictive Experiment Using the Independent Decision (Separate Source) Model

To further assess the usefulness of the model, it was employed to analyze the results of an experiment which involved changing conversational partners. Capitalizing upon the ability of this model to combine "individual speaker" parameters into new dyadic assemblies, we asked the following question:

How well can the model parameters obtained from one set of conversations predict the temporal patterns of another combination of the speakers, i.e., of a new set of dyadic assemblies? Suppose that speaker A talks to speaker B, and speaker C talks to speaker D, yielding two dyadic assemblies: A,B and C,D. Each of these conversations yields a set of parameters, the q_i and r_i of Equations (13) and (14) and the transition matrix $\tilde{P}$ of Equation (15). For convenience, we shall refer to the latter as the "expected $\tilde{P}$ matrices" under the independent decision hypothesis. The similarity of these expected $\tilde{P}$ matrices to the P matrices from which they were derived (the single-source model) indicates how well the model "fits" the dyadic assemblies A,B and C,D. This is shown above in Table IV-5 (left column).

Suppose, however, that we wish to *predict* the time patterns of the new dyadic assemblies A,C and B,D, using the individual parameters already obtained from conversations A,B and C,D. This can be accomplished by multiplying, according to Equation (15), the appropriate parameters obtained from A,B and C,D to generate new matrices which shall be designated the "predicted $\tilde{P}$ matrices." Would the predicted $\tilde{P}$ matrices thus obtained be similar to the P matrices derived from actual conversations A,C and B,D (the latter being the observed maximum likelihood matrices under the Markovian hypothesis)? Can we, in other words, predict the time patterns of a conversation by using, for each of its participants, model parameters estimated from his interaction with someone else?

This predictive power of the independent decision model was examined in the context of the second experiment described in Chapter III (Feldstein *et al.*, 1966). Recall that each of the subjects in that experiment engaged in three 40-minute dialogues, each of which took place on a different occasion (i.e., a different day) and with a *different partner*. There were, then, three occasions: the first and second same-sex occasions, i.e., occasions on which the conversations were between members of the same sex; and a mixed-sex occasion on which the partners were of opposite sex.[14] Parameter estimates were obtained for all these dialogues.

In general terms, we attempted to predict the conversational time patterns of each occasion using parameter estimates from each of the other two occasions. Thus, there were two sets of predicted matrices (considered replicates) for each occasion. For example, in order to predict the time patterns of the second same-sex occasion, the individual parameters derived from the first same-sex occasion were paired in the same way as the participants were paired on the second same-sex occasion and multiplied to generate predicted $\tilde{P}$ matrices. Similarly, the individual parameters derived from the mixed-sex occasion were appropriately paired to generate another set of predicted $\tilde{P}$ matrices. The conversational time patterns of the

---

[14] It may also be recalled that in addition to the fact that one of the three partners was a member of the opposite sex, the 40 minutes of conversation were divided into two conditions (see Chapter III). This information is not entirely germane to the issue before us, which is the predictive ability of the model. It is mentioned only to note that the effects of the conditions and change in partner sex were taken into account in statistically evaluating the model's predictive power.

first same-sex and mixed-sex occasions were predicted in like fashion.

To review the notation, we have four matrices for each conversation:

(1) The *observed* transition matrix P, which is the single-source model.

(2) The *expected* $\tilde{P}$ matrix, which is the independent decision model with all parameters estimated from the above mentioned matrix P. No prediction is involved here, the expected $\tilde{P}$ matrix merely being used to assess goodness of fit.

(3) The *predicted* $\tilde{P}$ matrix, concocted from parameter values which derive from other conversations, wherein the present participants were speaking to other partners.

(4) Another predicted $\tilde{P}$ matrix, a replicate of (3), with parameters derived from yet another set of dialogues.

We evaluated the model, within the context of this experiment, in two ways. These are illustrated diagrammatically in Figure IV-12. First we compared each expected $\tilde{P}$ matrix to the observed (single-source) P matrix from which it was derived (Figure IV-12, upper left). This is essentially a test of "fit" analogous to the one shown previously in Table IV-5. We also compared each predicted $\tilde{P}$

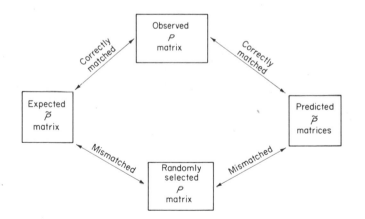

FIGURE IV-12. Matrix comparisons for the predictive study, carried out with the independent decision model.

matrix to its corresponding P matrix; there were two replicates of this prediction as described above and illustrated in Figure IV-12 (upper right). All comparisons were by means of the Neyman-Pearson statistic (NPS). As discussed earlier, we expected significant NPS levels in all comparisons due to the large numbers of observations. Our problem, as before, was to obtain some estimate of chance accuracy for the NPS, since the statistic is only meaningful when more than one model is being compared to the observed data. We did this by randomly mismatching the set of observed P matrices with both the expected and predicted $\tilde{P}$ matrices within each occasion and computing the NPS for each mismatched pair. These operations are depicted in Figure IV-12 (lower left and lower right). Our rationale was that if the fit of, or prediction by, the model was no better than chance, it should (on the average) account for the observed P matrix of *any* randomly selected pair of speakers as accurately as it accounted for the intended target dyad. The expectation, then, was that the average NPS of the correctly matched matrices would be significantly lower than that of the randomly mismatched matrices.

Analyses of variance were used to compare the NPSs. Each of the three occasions was analyzed separately; within each occasion the correctly matched and mismatched comparisons were also handled separately. In every analysis, the difference between the NPS of the correctly matched and mismatched matrices accounted for a significant portion of the total variance.[15] For those comparisons involving expected $\tilde{P}$ matrices (the test of fit in Figure IV-12, upper and lower left), F ratios were 78.08 (1,60 df) for the first same-sex occasion, 102.85 (1,59 df) for the second same-sex occasion, and 100.90 (1,60 df) for the mixed-sex occasion.

For those comparisons involving predicted $\tilde{P}$ matrices (Figure IV-12, upper and lower right), the F ratios were 13.18 (1,60 df), 19.43 (1,58 df), and 12.29 (1,59 df) for the first and second same-sex occasions and the mixed-sex occasion, respectively. Neither of the

---

[15] An unbiased estimate of the amount of variance accounted for by the difference is ϵ^2, which is equal to $(F - 1)df_n/(Fdf_n + df_d)$, where df_n is the degrees of freedom associated with the numerator of the F ratio, and df_d is the degrees of freedom associated with the denominator.

two replicates in this prediction was noticeably superior to the other. Table IV-7 represents the relevant descriptive statistics. Note that both types of randomly mismatched matrices, i.e., those involving expected $\tilde{P}$ and those involving predicted $\tilde{P}$ matrices, yielded very similar average NPSs, thereby lending some support for their use as estimates of chance accuracy.[16] Note also that the model fits the observed data somewhat better than it predicts them from another occasion, i.e., the expected $\tilde{P}$ NPSs are lower than predicted $\tilde{P}$ NPSs.

TABLE IV-7

MEANS (M) AND STANDARD DEVIATIONS (SD) OF NEYMAN-PEARSON STATISTIC FOR COMPARISON OF CORRECTLY MATCHED (CM) AND RANDOMLY MISMATCHED (MM) MATRICES ON EACH OCCASION

		Occasion		
		First same sex	Second same sex	Mixed sex
		Observed P Matrix vs. Expected $\tilde{P}$ Matrix		
CM	M	96.48	95.33	104.94
	SD	52.15	53.20	49.53
MM	M	394.23	378.25	368.76
	SD	209.76	180.83	169.02
		Observed P Matrix vs. Predicted $\tilde{P}$ Matrix		
CM	M	274.46	270.28	283.27
	SD	116.61	134.32	131.46
MM	M	389.23	365.83	387.48
	SD	192.04	164.28	165.50

The results suggest that, in terms of the Neyman-Pearson statistic, the independent decision model fits the observed data considerably better than chance. More importantly, they suggest that the model is capable of predicting the observed transition matrix with greater than chance accuracy.

---

[16] It might also be noted that the NPSs of the mismatched matrices are of the same order of magnitude as those of the normative model in Table IV-5, suggesting that the fit of the normative model is no better than chance.

EQUIVALENCE OF THE DESCRIPTIVE CLASSIFICATION AND THE STOCHASTIC MODELS

A unified framework for the descriptive classification and the Markov models, which have until now been treated as alternative approaches to the same data, is now presented. The synthesis takes the form of one additional mathematical model which embodies the major findings of the various experiments reported. The new model resolves several important issues that were left unsettled in previous chapters: (a) It remedies the worst defect of the four-state Markov model since it yields the individual pause and simultaneous speech parameters of the descriptive classification; (b) it explains why the four-state Markov model, which confounded these parameters for the two speakers, fit as well as it did; and (c) it revises the earlier taxonomy for the large class of conversations that can be categorized as free, spontaneous, or unstructured.

A brief restatement of the relative strengths and weaknesses of our two approaches to the rhythm of conversation will serve as an introduction. Recall that the parameters of the descriptive classification were behavioral units of the separate speakers that made intuitive sense, e.g., their average vocalization, pause, and switching pause lengths while they held the floor. These "individual" parameters were treated as conventional scores, and correlations between corresponding scores of the dialogue participants were the measures of interaction. A limitation of this taxonomy was that it possessed no strong consequences, being confined to the level of phenomenal description. For example, knowledge of the parameters of two individuals could not tell us how they shared the available conversational time. Having extracted, so to speak, the monologues from the context of dialogue, our initial approach was mute with respect to their recombination. Nevertheless, intensive study of the stability and modifiability of its parameters disclosed new empirical relationships such as the congruence of silences. It will presently become apparent that such observations were essential for a proper understanding of the stochastic models.

The alternative approach of probabilistic modeling seemed to transcend some of the foregoing limitations while breeding others. The Markov models disregarded the intuitive experience of dialogic rhythms and simply summarized the sequence of voice relay configurations in the form of a transition matrix. This scheme of data reduction, although very compact, initially obscured the behavioral categories which were of primary interest. Yet surprisingly the transition matrix yielded precisely those features of dialogic rhythm which were unobtainable from the descriptive classification. For example, the mean duration of holding the floor turned out to be a necessary consequence of the mathematical model. Further assumptions enabled us to make modest predictions of these features in speakers meeting for the first time.

As pointed out in the previous chapter, however, certain assumptions of the Markov model did violence to precisely those commonsense features of dialogue that any approach must satisfy. For example, it is apparent that a person has a higher probability of terminating a joint silence when he holds the floor than when he is in the listening mode. The four-state models of Chapter IV assert that these probabilities are the same. It is also apparent that interacting speakers may occasionally have quite different average pause durations; indeed, this was experimentally demonstrated in the experiments of Chapter III using the descriptive classification. The Markov models assert that a single silence state accounts for the silence distributions of both participants. When translated into terms of the descriptive classification, this implies that all four silence parameters, i.e., pauses and switching pauses of the two participants, must have the same mean duration. That this state of affairs may often occur was attested to by the consistently high correlations found among the four silence parameters. Yet, the fact that the correlations were less than perfect warns us of dialogues in which the silence patterns of the participants may be quite dissimilar. This important distinction was confounded in the Markov models previously explored, and posed the problem to which we now address ourselves.

I. Requirements for a Comprehensive Model of the Rhythm of Unstructured Dialogue[1]

When the discussion is restricted to unstructured dialogue, what are the essential requirements that must be met by a comprehensive model in order to account for the behavior of the speakers and for our previous findings?

(1) Separate vocalization parameters for the two speakers are required.

(2) Separate silence parameters for the two speakers[2] are required.

(3) Separate simultaneous speech parameters for the two speakers[3] are required.

(4) Each of these six parameters must describe a separate exponential distribution of "waiting times" in the respective state.

---

[1]With the demonstration in Chapter III that certain highly contrived conversations such as interviews may have specialized structures which are atypical, this discussion is based on the major findings of Studies 2 and 3 of that chapter in which the conversations were more spontaneous.

[2]Analysis by means of t tests of the difference between the average durations of pauses and switching pauses of Study 1 in Chapter III indicates that the differences are significant for each of the four subinterviews at the .01 level; for Study 2, which was unstructured relative to Study 1, the same comparisons were nonsignificant (no occasion nor condition within occasion yielded a significant t). Thus, a single silence parameter may suffice for each speaker in unstructured conversation, accounting for both his pauses and switching pauses.

[3]This is implied, although not used in the descriptive classification. The paucity of simultaneous speech led us to combine the distributions of both speakers. Yet it is clear that the speaker holding the floor has been "interrupted," while the other is "interrupting" in any simultaneous speech event.

(5) The model must distinguish which speaker has the floor at any given time (implied in 2 and 3).

(6) The frequency of speaker switches and mean duration of "floor time" must be derivable from the model.

(7) In addition to making those distinctions of the descriptive classification which were found to be essential for unstructured dialogue, the model should make intelligible the findings of the previous Markov models.

(8) Parameters must be derivable from the model which can be combined to predict the patterns of reconstituted dyads. In short, the model must provide a theory of *rhythmic interaction* which generates every essential feature of the temporal sequence.

A stochastic process is now described which meets all of the above requirements. It will have two versions, following the format of Chapter IV: a single-source and an independent decision version.

II. Six-State Single-Source Model

Throughout this monograph, the speaker switch has been the fundamental taxonomic criterion. Indeed, it was the keystone for the very definition of pause and switching pause in Chapters II and III. In Chapter IV the dyadic states were redefined as state $0 =$ both silent; state $1 = A$ speaks, B silent; state $2 = A$ silent, B speaks; state $3 =$ both speak. Viewing state 1 or 2 as an absorbing state of a Markov chain abstracted the speaker switch to a degree, but did not diminish its importance.

The speaker switch retains its central role in the present model as well. It is the basis for classification of the dyadic states into two sets, $\{Ai\}$ and $\{Bj\}$, with the letter indicating the speaker holding the floor and $i,j = 0,1,2,3$ as in the four-state classification. Recollecting that any speaker who vocalizes alone automatically has the floor, it is plain that states A2 and B1 are logically excluded. So we are left with two sets $\{Ai\}$ and $\{Bj\}$, where $i = 0,1,3$ and $j = 0,2,3$. These are the six states of the new model. They are defined as follows.

A0 = speaker A holds floor and there is joint silence
A1 = speaker A holds floor and vocalizes alone
A3 = speaker A holds floor and both vocalize

B0 = speaker B holds floor and there is joint silence
B2 = speaker B holds floor and vocalizes alone
B3 = speaker B holds floor and both vocalize

The state names were chosen to indicate a transduction, or mapping of the observed four-state sequence into another sequence in a six-state space. Note that there are now separate silence states, A0 and B0 (each of which combines pauses and switching pauses), and separate simultaneous speech states, A3 and B3, which were confounded in the four-state classification. The mapping is performed by an automaton which embodies the speaker switching rule; namely, "When any speaker vocalizes alone, he holds the floor." This "floor automaton" is depicted in Figure V-1. The

		Four-state input at time $t+1$			
		0	1	2	3
Speaker holding	A	A0	A1	B2	A3
floor at time t	B	B0	A1	B2	B3

FIGURE V-1. A diagram of the "floor automaton," i.e., the rules for transforming four-state sequences into six-state sequences. The entries represent the classification of the four dyadic states at time $t+1$ according to which speaker had the floor at time t.

row labels of the table indicate the speaker holding the floor at time t; the column labels of the table are the inputs to the automaton, i.e., the four states that may be observed at time $t+1$. The table entries show the reclassification of the four-state inputs into the six-state space at time $t+1$. (See legend Figure II-2.)

This floor automaton is a formalization of the psychological hypothesis underlying the descriptive classification of Chapters II and III. Recall that the speaker switching rule, which identifies the speaker holding the floor, was the basis for distinguishing the pauses and switching pauses of the respective speakers. The implied psychological hypothesis is that joint silences (and simultaneous speech), which are potentially competitive events, are assignable to the time domain of one or the other participant.

The reclassification of the input sequence by the floor automaton presents us with a new stochastic process for which a transition matrix is computed, exactly as was performed for the four-state sequence in Chapter IV.

The transition matrix, M, for the six-state model is shown in Equation (1).

$$M = \begin{bmatrix} m_{11} & m_{12} & m_{13} & 0 & m_{15} & 0 \\ m_{21} & m_{22} & m_{23} & 0 & m_{25} & 0 \\ m_{31} & m_{32} & m_{33} & 0 & m_{35} & 0 \\ 0 & m_{42} & 0 & m_{44} & m_{45} & m_{46} \\ 0 & m_{52} & 0 & m_{54} & m_{55} & m_{56} \\ 0 & m_{62} & 0 & m_{64} & m_{65} & m_{66} \end{bmatrix} \qquad (1)$$

States A0 through B3 above are numbered 1 through 6 to simplify the subscript notation, but the two notations will be used interchangeably. The elements m_{ij} are the conditional probabilities of moving from state i at time t to state j at time $t+1$ $(i,j = 1,2,...,6)$. M is the maximum likelihood matrix of a six-state Markov chain.[4] Its stationary distribution of state probabilities is the vector $[p(A0),$ $p(A1), p(A3), p(B0), p(B2), p(B3)]$. Since we have decided to number these states sequentially from 1 to 6, the state probabilities will also be expressed as the vector $p(i)$, with $i = 1,2,...,6$. The zero elements show the logically excluded transitions, since the only communication between subsets $\{Ai\}$ and $\{Bj\}$ is via a speaker switch, i.e., a transition to state B2 if the process was in $\{Ai\}$, or to A1 if the process was in $\{Bj\}$, where $i = 0,1,3$ and $j = 0,2,3$.

M summarizes the entire sequence of voice relay configurations exactly as did the matrices in Chapter IV, except that state assignment cannot begin until one speaker is known to have the floor. Thus, in contrast to the four-state models of Chapter IV but consistent with the descriptive classification, a dialogue cannot begin with a joint silence or simultaneous speech. The moment one speaker vocalizes alone, the holder of the floor is identified and accumulation of the six-state frequency matrix begins. This fre-

[4]Definitions of maximum likelihood matrix and its stationary distribution are given in Chapter IV.

quency matrix is shown in diagrammatic form in Figure V-2 to illustrate several interesting features of its structure.

$$
F = \begin{bmatrix} \begin{bmatrix} & A & \end{bmatrix} & \begin{matrix} 0 \\ 0 \\ 0 \end{matrix} & \begin{bmatrix} C \end{bmatrix} & \begin{matrix} 0 \\ 0 \\ 0 \end{matrix} \\ \begin{matrix} 0 \\ 0 \\ 0 \end{matrix} & \begin{bmatrix} D \end{bmatrix} & \begin{matrix} 0 \\ 0 \\ 0 \end{matrix} & \begin{bmatrix} & B & \end{bmatrix} \end{bmatrix}
$$

FIGURE V-2. A diagrammatic representation of Equation (1) which partitions the matrix into submatrices (A and B) of the dyadic behavior that occurs while each speaker (A or B) has the floor, and into vectors (C and D) of the switches between the submatrices.

F is a supermatrix composed of two 3 by 3 submatrices, A and B, and two 3-element column vectors, C and D. Submatrices A and B contain all the transitions possible while the respective speakers hold the floor. These are transitions *within* subsets $\{Ai\}$ and $\{Bj\}$, the mutually exclusive time domains of the interaction. C and D are speaker switching vectors, each composed of the three transitions by means of which a speaker can gain the floor, thus moving the process into his own time domain. They are the link between $\{Ai\}$ and $\{Bj\}$. Note that the sum of the frequencies of C is the number of times speaker A gains the floor and can differ by at most 1 from the sum of the frequencies of D. Thus, the switching vectors of F each contain the exact number of speaker switches in the dialogue, an interactive feature which could only be estimated from the four-state transition matrices by calculation of absorption probabilities. The total number of counts in states A0, A1, and A3 (the sum of the first 3 rows of F) is the total floor time for speaker A. This total divided by the total counts in C is the average utterance duration for speaker A. Analogous calculations are performed for speaker B. Once again, these are not estimates but definitions.

When the dialogue ends, matrix F is normalized precisely as in the four-state models. Each element is divided by its row sum to yield the stochastic transition matrix M of Equation (1).

Another way of conceptualizing the states of this model is in terms of the symmetry of the voice relay configurations. States 1 and 2 are asymmetrical configurations in the four-state model. They are identical to A1 and B2 in the six-state model, which offers no new information about them apart from the fact that there are now six rather than four ways of reaching them. The symmetrical states 0 and 3 of the four-state model are each subdivided in the six-state space which reclassifies them on the basis of a reasonable psychological hypothesis: that B is "listening" during A0 and "interrupting" during A3; that A is listening during B0 and interrupting during B3. This stochastic process must pass through an asymmetrical state in moving between the symmetrical states of the two speakers; A0 or A3 cannot be adjacent to B0 or B3. This again is merely a statement of the speaker switching rule.

III.   Justification for Extra States

Is the six-state model necessary? It claims that *it really matters who has the floor*, that the mean pause, switching pause, and simutaneous speech of a speaker may differ widely from those of his partner. If possession of the floor were a meaningless distinction, the relations of Equations (2) and (3) would hold. (Recall that the six-state subscripts run from 1 to 6, whereas the four-state subscripts of Chapter IV run from 0 to 3.)

$$\text{Six-state} \qquad \text{Four-state}$$

$$m_{1i} = m_{4j} = \qquad p_{0k} \qquad (2)$$
$$m_{3i} = m_{6j} = \qquad p_{3k} \qquad (3)$$

$$(i,j,k = 1,4,0;\ 2,2,1;\ 5,5,2;\ 3,6,3)$$

These equations show that the transition probabilities from joint silence to any given state are the same, regardless of which speaker is pausing, and that the transition probabilities from simultaneous speech to any given state are the same, regardless of which speaker is "interrupting." These equalities define the conditions for *lumpability* of the states of a Markov chain. If a chain is lumpable, certain states can be combined (not discriminated), and the chain remains Markovian. An illustration will make this clear.

Suppose we wished to model the combined distributions of silence, without regard to the speaker who has the floor. The transition (conditional) probabilities to be combined for this pooled silence distribution are m_{11} and m_{44} of M. But each of these ij transitions must first be appropriately weighted by the chance of ever being in its respective state i, which is $p(i)$ of the stationary distribution of M. Thus, the absolute probability of a $1 \rightarrow 1$ transition is $p(1)m_{11}$, and of a $4 \rightarrow 4$ transition is $p(4)m_{44}$. These values may now be added and converted to the desired conditional probability for the pooled distribution by dividing by the sum of the state probabilities, to get

$$\frac{p(1)m_{11} + p(4)m_{44}}{p(1) + p(4)}$$

It is apparent from this expression that if $m_{11} = m_{44}$, the m_{ij} can be factored out and all the state probabilities cancel. This is the essence of the condition of lumpability. It would have to be true for all the other transitions from either A0 or B0 to any given state, for example, to state A1. In this case we would want to combine m_{12} and m_{42} of M. The desired transition probability would then be

$$\frac{p(1)m_{12} + p(4)m_{42}}{p(1) + p(4)}$$

Again, if $m_{12} = m_{42}$, the state probabilities would cancel. In dialogic terms this means that speaker A had the identical probability of starting to talk after a silence whether or not he had the floor.[5] In the former, he would be resuming following his own pause; in the latter, he would be initiating a new utterance following a switching pause. If the pair of silence states and the pair of simultaneous speech states are lumpable, there is no justification for separating them, since the six-state process is simply equivalent to the four-state process of the previous chapter. And there would be no point in knowing which speaker had the floor, which would also imply

---

[5] In reality, m_{12} is four times greater, on the average, than m_{42} in unstructured dialogue.

that the separate silence parameters of the descriptive classification were redundant.

The test of this assertion of lumpability is to construct the implied model by substituting the observed four-state transition probabilities p_{ij} in matrix M. The likelihoods of the six-state process and the lumped model are then compared statistically exactly as in Chapter IV. The substitutions indicated in Equations (2) and (3) were, therefore, performed. The result was matrix M' of Equation (4) which is properly lumpable, since combining the two silence states and the two simultaneous speech states, respectively, yields the four-state Markov model.

$$
M' = \begin{bmatrix}
p_{00} & p_{01} & p_{03} & 0 & p_{02} & 0 \\
p_{10} & p_{11} & p_{13} & 0 & p_{12} & 0 \\
p_{30} & p_{31} & p_{33} & 0 & p_{32} & 0 \\
0 & p_{01} & 0 & p_{00} & p_{02} & p_{03} \\
0 & p_{21} & 0 & p_{20} & p_{22} & p_{23} \\
0 & p_{31} & 0 & p_{30} & p_{32} & p_{33}
\end{bmatrix}
\tag{4}
$$

The question can now be posed: Do the stochastic processes defined by M and M' differ significantly? If so, then it matters who has the floor and the four-state processes of Chapter IV do indeed represent a confounded state space. To test this, two separate groups of four subjects each engaged in spontaneous one-hour conversations. All were female college students, native-born, paid volunteers. Each subject spoke to the three other members of her group, yielding 12 hours of dialogue. Thus, there were eight subjects, each participating in 3 of the 12 conversations. However, no two dyadic assemblies were the same. Physical position at the two microphones was randomized. Computation of the Neyman-Pearson statistic for each of the 12 dialogues yielded values ranging from 71 to 829 with a median of 465, a fact not in itself interpretable for reasons given in Chapter IV. It can be asserted, however, that whereas none of the six-state matrices is absolutely lumpable (a value greater than 28 is beyond chance), many of them are approximately so. This is attributed to the empirical phenomenon of "silence congruence," which explains why the four-state models which lost track of possession of the floor, were nevertheless able to yield excellent estimates of speaker switching. The justification for the larger state space must be its ability to account for the cases which are clearly not lumpable and its superiority in other respects.

IV.   The Information in the Six-State Matrix

We now claim that all the information contained in the descriptive classification is also contained in the six-state stochastic matrix. To show this, each of the previously stated requirements for a comprehensive model will be taken up in turn and examined in the 12 conversations used for the lumpability tests.

Examining matrix M of Equation (1) we see that the main diagonal is composed of six parameters, each describing the probability of remaining in one of the states. They are classified in Table V-1. Since each parameter will be shown to describe a separate exponential distribution, the mean duration[6] in any state is given by $1/(1-m_{ii})$.

TABLE V-1

A CATEGORIZATION OF THE PARAMETERS OF THE SIX-STATE, SINGLE-SOURCE MODEL IN TERMS OF THE PARAMETERS OF THE DESCRIPTIVE CLASSIFICATION

	Speaker	
Parameter	A	B
Silence	m_{11}	m_{44}
Vocalization	m_{22}	m_{55}
Simultaneous speech	m_{66}	m_{33}

The vocalization parameters pose no problem, since transition probabilities m_{22} and m_{55} are identical with those of both the descriptive taxonomy and four-state Markov model. Their correlation with the vocalization parameters of the descriptive classification is given in Table V-2.

---

[6]See footnote 1, Chapter III.

It is clear that m_{22} and m_{55} can substitute for the vocalization parameter of the descriptive classification.[7] As found in Chapter III, there is no correlation in unstructured dialogue between the vocalization lengths of the two speakers.

TABLE V-2

INTERCORRELATION OF VOCALIZATION PARAMETERS $(N = 12)^a$

	V_A	m_{55}	V_B
m_{22}	.96	.05	−.08
V_A	−	.04	−.13
m_{55}	−	−	.92

^{a}V stands for the average duration of vocalizations; A and B refer to the speakers.

Proceeding to the silence parameters m_{11} and m_{44}, they describe, respectively, each speaker's silence while he holds the floor. The single silence parameter for each speaker pools the events which were previously designated as pause and switching pause. One assumption of the model, therefore, is that the pause and switching pause parameters for a speaker derive from the same silence distribution, the only one operative for him while he holds the floor. To see whether this assumption is justified, the correlations of m_{11} and m_{44} with the silence parameters of the descriptive classification for which they must account, are examined in Table V-3.

The nine correlations in the upper right area of the matrix show the correlation of silence parameters *between* speakers. Although these coefficients are high, attesting to the high degree of silence congruence in unstructured conversation, they are uniformly lower than the six *within*-speaker correlations in the upper left and lower right portions of the matrix. The latter show the relation, for each speaker, between the single silence parameter from matrix M and the two silence parameters of the descriptive classification;

---

[7]A few very long vocalizations are not accounted for by the Markov model but do enter into the calculation of V_A or V_B.

m_{11} and m_{44} are almost perfectly correlated with the two types of silence. In fact, there is a lower correlation between pause and switching pause than between each of these and the six-state parameter.[8]

TABLE V-3

INTERCORRELATIONS OF SILENCE PARAMETERS $(N = 12)^a$

	P_A	SwP_A		m_{44}	P_B	SwP_B
m_{11}	.98	.98		.79	.78	.69
P_A	—	.94		.81	.79	.70
SwP_A	—	—		.73	.77	.62
m_{44}	—	—		—	.96	.96
P_B	—	—		—	—	.86

$^a P$ and SwP stand for the average durations of pauses and switching pauses, respectively; A and B refer to the speakers. The correlations between pauses and switching pauses were of the order of .6 in Chapter III using a larger number of subjects. With an N of 12 ($df = 10$), an r must be equal to or greater than .58 to be significant at the .05 level.

It is clear to this point that the major information of the descriptive classification with respect to its vocalization, pause, and switching pause parameters are contained in matrix M.

The remaining parameters m_{33} and m_{66} describe two essentially different categories of simultaneous speech, depending upon which speaker has the floor. The implication is that the simultaneous speaker who does not have the floor is in some sense "interrupting." An event contributing to m_{33} consists of the vocalization onset by speaker B during continuous vocalization of speaker A, such that the latter has held the floor. Parameter m_{66} accounts for the converse situation.

Because, for our data, the two types of simultaneous speech were pooled to form a single histogram, the validity of assigning these matrix elements to the individual speakers cannot be assessed from present data. The proportionality constant, SS_{A+B}, of the pooled

[8]In the lumped four-state process shown in Equation (4), the single confounded silence parameter p_{00} must account for all silences of both speakers.

simultaneous speech histogram can, however, be predicted from M as a value λ such that

$$\lambda = \frac{p(3)m_{33} + p(6)m_{66}}{p(3) + p(6)}$$

The correlation coefficient of λ with SS_{A+B} for the 12 conversations is .99.

V.   Mean "Floor Time" between Speaker Switches

The number of speaker switches and the mean time that each speaker holds the floor between switches could be computed from the four-state matrices of the preceding chapter only as a consequence of the Markov hypothesis. In contrast, the states of the six-state, single-source process acknowledge the holder of the floor, so these phenomena are simply counted rather than estimated.[9] The frequencies of speaker switches are the same for both speakers and are given directly by the switching vectors of F in Figure V-2. The average duration of holding the floor is accurately obtained from the total frequencies in a given speaker's time domain, e.g., in $A+D$ divided by the frequency of switches. (This result must be multiplied, of course, by the real time value of each sample.)

VI.   Six-State Silence Distribution

In the previous chapter, the four-state Markov model was used to fit the frequency distributions of silence and vocalization durations. These were exponential distributions. The six-state single-source prediction of vocalization distributions is by definition identical to that of the four-state model. Thus, if the larger state space is to improve the fit of the distributions over that of the four-state model, it must be seen in the effect of separate silence parameters on individual silence distributions. Figure V-3 shows the difference in

---

[9]This is not the case, however, for the six-state independent decision model discussed subsequently; its unique stationary distribution requires computation of speaker switches and mean floor time as a consequence of the model.

one such fit, selected from a dialogue in which there was a large discrepancy between six-state silence parameters m_{11} and m_{44}. In such a conversation, the four-state silence parameter p_{00} would be confounded and would yield a poorer fit for the silence distribution of one or both participants. The relevant equations are derived for speaker A only; analogous computations will be obvious for speaker B.

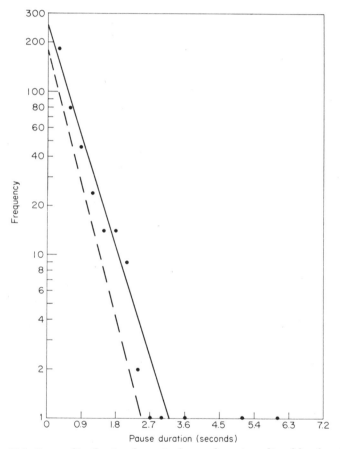

FIGURE V-3. Pause distribution for a single speaker as predicted by the six- and four-state models. The solid line is the six-state prediction; the dashed line is the four-state prediction, and the plotted points are the observed frequencies. The distribution is derived from a dialogue lasting 60 minutes.

To predict the pause distribution for speaker A, the boundaries of the pause event must be considered. State 1 must be bounded by vocalizations of A such that he keeps the floor. Equation (1) indicates that there are but two ways to enter state 1 for the first time (via 2 or 3), and but two ways of leaving it such that speaker A vocalizes (also 2 or 3). The desired sequences are, therefore, 2,1,...,1,2; 2,1,...,1,3; 3,1,...,1,2; and 3,1,...,1,3. Repetition of state 1 prolongs the pause. Thus, the probability that speaker A pauses for duration L is given by

$$Pr(\text{pause } L) = [p(2)t_{21} + p(3)t_{31}]t_{11}^{L-1}(t_{12} + t_{13})$$

Substitution of t_{15} for $(t_{12} + t_{13})$ in this equation predicts the distribution of switching pauses.

VII. Six-State Independent Decision Model

A reduction in the number of parameters of the six-state process from 18 to 12 can be achieved by means of an independent decision hypothesis, exactly as was done with the four-state model of the previous chapter. There are four nonzero elements per row of matrix M in Equation (1). Since each row sums to one, it is specified by three of its elements; six rows with three parameters each specify the entire matrix. The additional independent decision hypothesis is the same as in Chapter IV.

Let
  q_i = probability that speaker A vocalizes at time $t+1$ given dyadic
       state i at time t

  r_i = probability that speaker B vocalizes at time $t+1$ given dyadic
       state i at time t
where
  $i = (A0, A1, A3, B0, B2, B3) = (1, 2, ..., 6)$

Under this hypothesis, an approximation to matrix M can be generated using only 6 parameters per speaker; q_i and r_i for each row i are appropriately multiplied as in Chapter IV to yield the six-state independent decision matrix. This computation will not be shown, but it may be observed that the four-state independent decision model of Chapter IV is simply this six-state independent decision model under the special restrictions of the lumpability hypothesis of Equations (2) and (3). The six-state independent decision model also offers the opportunity for recombination of speaker parameters into new dyadic assemblies. As illustrated with the four-state independent decision model in the experiment which concludes the previous chapter, predictions of new interactions are thereby possible using parameters derived from other dialogues. The conceptual superiority of the six-state over the four-state model suggests that such predictions could be improved if analyses were repeated in terms of the six-state independent decision hypothesis. The analysis will not be repeated here, however.

CHAPTER VI

SUMMARY AND FUTURE DIRECTIONS

Our research was based upon the assumption that dialogic rhythms constitute a fruitful source of information, not only about the mechanisms of conversation, but also about the participants and their relationships to each other. This summary reviews what has been learned and how the findings might fit into a theoretical framework of human communication.

We began by committing ourselves to automated interaction chronography of vocal interaction, that is, to a decision (a) to restrict the source of information about a conversation to the behavior of a pair of voice-actuated relays which treat any sound above threshold as equivalent, and (b) to restrict the data analysis to that which could be completely performed by a digital computer. The former restriction is a profound abstraction of the conversation, deleting virtually everything which is considered intrinsic to the behavior by the layman. The second restriction precludes any inference in the data analysis that is not explicitly stated in the computer program. Having thus reduced the richness of dialogue to at least manageable proportions by filtering out everything that could conceivably motivate a person to engage in it, the computer program which would embody our theory was defined. In this task, we proceeded from both theoretical and empirical considerations.

Theoretically, the evidence from first language learning, from anthropology, and from various interpersonal or transactional theories of psychology suggested that a conversation is developmentally prior to its component monologues. The frame of reference

113

VI. SUMMARY AND FUTURE DIRECTIONS

had a definite influence upon the perceived research task which, from this viewpoint, seemed to require the decomposition of dialogue into its respective individual behaviors. One could have proceeded in the opposite direction, namely, to study monologues and to try to fathom how they might be concatenated into conversations. We believe the choice was a fortunate one. From a general systems theory viewpoint, insight into systems at a given level of complexity may often be obtained from examination of levels both higher and lower in the hierarchy of organization. Indeed, it is suggested in the first two chapters that multilogues may be the more general case of dialogues, and, at a lower level, that one can sense the operation of certain neural attention mechanisms in the "politeness rules" of social conversation.

Empirical considerations also entered into the development of the computer program. In scanning the sound–silence sequence of a dialogue (see Figure II-2), certain patterns force themselves upon us. There are silences with different boundary conditions, periods of simultaneous speech, etc. Some of these are easily seen as pauses, switching pauses, and unilateral vocalizations. Others, especially those involving simultaneous speech, are so complex that some rule is called for to bring order out of the chaos. The "speaker switching rule" used in defining possession of the floor (Definition 2, Chapter II) resolves, by fiat, all these complex patterns that defy classification. This fact, in addition to the intuitive feeling that no matter how briefly a speaker vocalizes alone he "gains the floor," made the speaker switch the key phenomenon of the descriptive classification. It handled traffic at just those junctures (change of speaker, points of rapid interchange, and simultaneous speech) where the interface between the component monologues occurs. This having been accomplished, the descriptive classification was codified as shown in Chapter II. The taxonomy is composed of five empirically defined categories: (1) *vocalization,* (2) *pause,* (3) *switching pause,* (4) *speaker switch,* and (5) *simultaneous speech,* each defined symmetrically for the two speakers. These are transactional definitions; variation in either speaker's pattern can cause the reclassification of even an invariant pattern of the other.

One theoretical implication of the transactional definition of all categories is that if one dialogue participant is silent (or absent), the classification becomes simply appropriate to a monologue, i.e., there are *pauses* and *vocalizations* for one speaker, but no *speaker switches, switching pauses,* or *simultaneous speech.* Another implication is that the investigation of multilogues merely requires a straightforward extension of the instrumentation, without modification of the descriptive classification.

We found, as did previous investigators using similar classifications, that the empirical distributions of the temporal categories are approximately exponential. The importance of this finding is that it suggested that the temporal structure of dialogue may be described in terms of certain types of stochastic processes, a suggestion explored in detail in Chapters IV and V.

There is only a loose correspondence of the categories to the units of descriptive linguistics. The average duration of *vocalizations* appears roughly to approximate that of phonemic clauses. It is more difficult to compare *switching pauses* and *pauses* to juncture and hesitation pauses, the definitions of which entail syntactical considerations. However, some preliminary findings with respect to the relation between silence and syntax are discussed at the end of Chapter III.

The major aim in Chapter III is to demonstrate, through the analyses of experimentally elicited dialogues, the plausibility of the particular description of the temporal flow of dialogue developed previously. It is shown that the parameters of that description allow us to distinguish at least two types of dialogue: the interview, and that class having relatively minimal formal structure, i.e., "natural" or "ordinary" conversations.

For example, our interview studies produced too little simultaneous speech for reliable assessment. The incidence of this category increased to the values shown only in unstructured dialogue (see Appendix D). This would seem to be one important distinction between structured and unstructured dialogue. Another is that the correlation between pauses and switching pauses is significantly different for these two types of conversation, being higher in the unstructured type. The implication of these findings is that a completely automated system has been shown capable of making a discrimination between a set of interviews and a set of unstructured conversations on the basis of the parameters of the classification and without being given information about the roles of the participants.

The parameters appear under certain explicit conditions to be quite reliable and to be capable of differentiating the temporal styles of individuals and of pairs of individuals. The parameters are modifiable. They are capable of reflecting certain kinds of changes in the environmental and psychological contexts within which dialogues occur. To illustrate such modifiability, we demonstrated that the values of the parameters change when the speakers cannot see each other, and as a response to induced psychological stress.

A good way of summarizing these findings is to say that the pacing of conversational interactions is (a) characteristic of the speakers involved, (b) stable within any particular conversation, and (c) consistent from one conversation to the next for the same two speakers. At the same time, the temporal pattern of an individual is capable of modifying, and of being modified by that of his conversational partner to such an extent that (except for vocalizations) it need not remain stable from conversation to conversation when the successive conversations involve different partners and different topics. Of interest here is a study by Meltzer, Hayes, and Shellenberger (1966) which found that the duration of "vocal sequences" (comparable to vocalizations) showed no individual consistency over interactions that involved changes of partners and topics. However, their interactions were elicited from three-person groups. Thus, for each participant, each successive interaction involved *two* new partners rather than the one new partner encountered by our subjects. Whether it was this further change that destroyed the stability of so seemingly stable a parameter as vocalizations is difficult to evaluate without a replication.[1] Barring

---

[1]There are other sources of variance that may contribute to the unreliability reported by Meltzer *et al.* (1966). The fact that their analog-to-digital conversion was at a rate of 375 samples per minute as compared with the 200 samples per minute utilized for the research reported in Chapter III would not seem to be an adequate explanation of the discrepancy between their results and ours. The reliabilities reported by Welkowitz and Feldstein (1969) are comparable to those reported herein even though their instrument sampled at a rate of 600 per minute. However, one important similarity of the latter instrument to that described in this monograph is that both utilize the same time constant, i.e., one which yields a temporal description comparable to the pattern perceived by the naive human listener (see Appendix A for further details). Thus, in spite of a threefold increase in sampling rate, the average parameter durations observed by Welkowtiz and Feldstein are strikingly

such changes, however, the parameters of an individual's temporal style tend to remain consistent even across different conversational contexts, although they are also capable of indexing the fact that the contexts are different.

On the other hand, it cannot be denied that many of an individual's everyday conversations involve different partners and topics. Are we then to say that the consistency of an individual's temporal parameters, so fragile in the face of multiple topics and partners, is an artifact of the experimental designs in which these variables were specifically controlled? The findings seem to suggest something else, namely, that consistency of time patterns is a function of particular human relationships which, when prolonged as in real life, do indeed tend to revolve about a limited set of conversational topics appropriate to the role structure of the specific dyad. Where there is a high expectancy regarding the appropriate role structure, an individual's parameters might show stability even in the face of multiple partners and topics. This remains to be investigated.

To summarize our experiments, the findings lend support to Chapple's (1939) notion that the timing of interpersonal interactions (among which he included nonverbal interactions) could provide the behavioral data needed for a reliable assessment of personality. While the validity of the inferences he drew has yet to be demonstrated experimentally, the isomorphism they imply is seductively simple. With respect only to verbal exchanges, is the man who characteristically uses short bursts of speech (short vocalizations) and short pauses—a clipped, staccato way of talking—a chronically impatient individual? Is the person who tends to do the most talking the more dominant individual? Is the degree of reliability of an individual's temporal style related to that of his other modes of behavior? Within the context of this concern about personalogical inferences there are many such questions worth raising, although their investigation reaches beyond the scope of this monograph.

---

similar to those reported herein. Since Meltzer *et al.* give no information about this important aspect of their instrumentation, the difference between the reliabilities of our experiments and theirs cannot be properly evaluated. Their use of bone microphones is still another source of variance that makes comparison difficult.

The descriptive classification employed in Chapters II and III decomposes the temporal sequence into an empirically defined set of categories. But having accomplished this, we found ourselves in the proverbial predicament of "all the king's horses and all the king's men." In short, the taxonomy is devoid of rules for reconstituting the temporal sequence from the derived parameter values, nor are rules provided for using the parameter values to predict future conversational patterns of the participants. Chapters IV and V attempt to cope with this lack.

The point of departure of Chapter IV is not the categories of the descriptive classification, but rather the sequence of four dyadic states produced by the analog to digital conversion of the gross vocalization pattern of conversation. This sequence is viewed as a stochastic process with a one-step (300 milliseconds) contingency. The Markov chain thus defined is first illustrated for monologue to bring out certain properties of the model with a manageable number of states. The four-state "single-source" model for dialogue is then defined. This sequence of monologue preceding dialogue had a purely didactic purpose. Theoretically the monologue models are special cases of the dialogue models, i.e., the latter reduce to the former when one speaker is silent or absent. The four-state model does not take account of "possession of the floor." It utilizes a single confounded silence state and a single confounded simultaneous speech state. It is, nevertheless, shown to account remarkably well for certain dyadic phenomena which are unobtainable from the descriptive classification presented in Chapters II and III, e.g., mean intervals between speaker switches. The four-state, single-source matrix also permits an approximate fit to other parameters of the descriptive classification, e.g., pause, switching pause, and vocalization distributions.

A separate source model is then developed which is more appealing in that it assumes two separate but related speakers, rather than a single dyadic source. Although it fits less well than does the single-source model, this independent decision model has the advantage of "individual" parameters which are capable of recombination to predict other interactions in which a speaker has not yet participated. An experimental assessment demonstrated that the model is capable of predicting such interactions with an accuracy significantly greater than chance.

However, the four-state independent decision model shares a major defect with the single-source model in that, as a special case of the latter, it also neglects to notice possession of the floor. Its single silence state similarly confounds four types of silence, i.e., the pauses and switching pauses of both speakers (and its single simultaneous speech state is also confounded). Thus, the distributions of these silence categories must all have identical means, whether generated by the single-source *or* the independent decision model. In this sense, both four-state models may obscure some of the detail inherent in the exponential distributions of silence categories presented in Chapter II. This shortcoming is dealt with in Chapter V.

A stochastic model is proposed in Chapter V which satisfies all the requirements of unstructured dialogue which were discovered in experiments with the descriptive classification. It is a "six-state, single-source" model which retains the mathematical power of the models of the prior chapter, although circumventing some of their unpleasant assumptions, namely, that silence and simultaneous speech are unitary dyadic states and that it is not necessary to discriminate the speaker who holds the floor. In mathematical terms, these assumptions mean that the six-state process is lumpable, i.e., that the participants' silence and simultaneous speech parameters are identical, and that these four states may be combined into two without loss of information, yielding the four-state model of Chapter IV. Statistical tests of the lumpability hypothesis showed it to be somewhat poorer than the six-state, single-source model, under the hypothesis that the latter is Markovian. Nevertheless, the paucity of simultaneous speech and the empirically high correlation between silence parameters of the interacting speakers render the process (in some sense) approximately lumpable. Results of the previous chapter showing reasonable predictions obtainable with the four-state model, which simply neglects possession of the floor, thereby become intelligible.

The six-state model has a separate source (independent decision) version which is completely analogous to the four-state separate source model (Jaffe, 1967). It offers individual parameters for use in predictive studies of recombined speakers. The six-state models of Chapter V demonstrate the complete equivalence of the Markov chain models and the descriptive classification when the distinction made by the latter between pauses and switching pauses is omitted.

To summarize the stochastic modeling chapters, it has been observed for many years that sound and silence durations in speech are exponentially distributed. Indeed, Mosteller (1949) modeled the rhythm of monologue as alternate random choices from a pair of such distributions. What we have added is

(a) the observation that Mosteller's simulation result implies a Markovian structure in speech rhythms,

(b) a theory of the way in which two such Markov sources might combine to produce the rhythm of a dialogue,

(c) an algorithm for deciding whether hypothesized "unobserved" states of the stochastic process are justified statistically (see Appendix C), and

(d) a demonstration, since we show the equivalence of the six-state model and the descriptive classification in unstructured dialogues, of the psychological validity of the parameters of the Markov model.

With respect to the last point, (d), the six-state model parameters would obviously reproduce the results of the experiments of Chapter III, although these studies were analyzed in terms of the descriptive classification. What advantage accrues from a restatement of that classification as a Markovian theory? The first is the combinatory capability of the independent decision models and the fact that the interaction hypothesis is not simply additive. A theory is provided which permits the prediction of new *sequences* of interaction behavior using parameters derived from other interactions. Indeed, the Markov process can be used as a simulation model to generate actual sequences for specific purposes, e.g., to study the effects of altering parameter values of the model. Since we find the Markovian property throughout our data, variations in the rhythm of dialogue can then be attributed to such altered parameter values in a relatively invariant mathematical structure.

Second, the stochastic model furnishes a critical tool for the examination of research performed by others. In Chapter I the seeming contradiction between the short range constraints of our Markov models and the long range constraints reported by other investigators was noted. Conceiving of sound–silence sequences of speech as the output of a stochastic process raises the well known possibility that humans are prone to detect rhythmic phenomena in random fluctuations.

Yet another advantage of the Markov models is their heuristic function. For example, one of the most striking findings of this research was the tendency for interacting speakers to match the average pause durations which they employ as they alternately hold the floor. One senses an empathetic or imitative mechanism in this mutual pacing which, conceived as "silence matching," would have to rely on rather long-term memory. That is, the speaker must recall the pause durations to which he was exposed as the previous listener, perhaps for several utterance cycles back in the conversation. In terms of the six-state, independent decision model, however, each listener's activity is described by three distinct parameters. Depending upon whether the speaker holding the floor was vocalizing alone or pausing, or whether he (the listener) was attempting to interrupt, these parameters describe his independent probabilities of vocalizing in the next instant. Thus, the Markov hypothesis suggests a continuous decision process by the listener as well as the speaker holding the floor, both based upon very short-term memory of their joint configuration. A mechanism is implied by means of which both participants continuously regulate the silence durations of the speaker holding the floor. From this point of view the observed "silence congruence" is achieved by a variety of mutually offsetting adjustments, and the underlying dynamics become a fertile field for future investigation. Assignment of parameters to the "listening state" also suggests points of articulation with contemporary notions about the decoding of spoken language, as does the fact that the durations of pauses and switching pauses are similar in unstructured dialogue.

As another example of the heuristic value of the stochastic modeling, consider the interesting question posed by the exponential distributions of sound and silence durations which must be produced by a language-generating process which cannot itself be Markovian (Miller *et al.*, 1964). Conceivable mechanisms to explain this remain a task for the future, but their outlines are beginning to be formulated (Anderson & Jaffe, 1970).

Finally, the greatest advantage which accrues from a restatement of the descriptive classification as a stochastic process is the applicability of all the existing machinery of Markov chain theory to the derivation of mathematical consequences of the model which then lend themselves to empirical test.

APPENDIX A[1]

THE AUTOMATIC VOCAL TRANSACTION ANALYZER (AVTA)

AVTA is a two-channel speech detector and analog to digital converter designed to bridge the gap between live or tape-recorded interviews and an on-line digital computer. As a two-channel A to D converter it has much in common with other interaction chronograph systems in which the subjects' behaviors are tracked either manually or by means of a voice-actuated relay. Its unique feature is a network which electronically cancels the unintended "spill" of each speaker's voice into the other's microphone. This special feature confines each speaker's voice to one channel of the audio-tape even though ordinary microphones are used and the speakers are conversing at close range in a face-to-face situation. This particular feature eliminates the need to separate the participants via isolation booths, or by use of throat or bone microphones, or other such solutions to the "cross-talk" problem. The goal was, of course, maintenance of as natural a dialogic context as possible. The circuitry will be presented in more detail below, but some theoretical considerations are required as an introduction.

The implications of the research presented throughout the monograph must ultimately be referred back to the physical events encoded by AVTA. This problem was considered in Chapter II where our computerized classification categories were found to be confounding certain linguistic events. But one may ask, what is a

---

[1]Appendixes A and B are based primarily on the following two publications: Cassotta, Feldstein, and Jaffe (1964), and Cassotta, Jaffe, Feldstein, and Moses (1964).

speech detector? The most sophisticated analysis of this problem from the point of view of our type of data was performed by Brady (1968, 1969). In the latter reference (Section 1.2, p. 5) he gives the following definition: "A speech detector is a rule which transforms speech into on–off patterns.[2]"

We take this to mean that the presence or absence of speech, the basic datum, is a complex function of at least six independently controllable features of the AVTA system:

(1) The intensity of the vocal signal
(2) The background noise during the conversation
(3) The threshold setting for voice relay closure
(4) Smoothing of the analog waveform by the time constant for relay opening
(5) The sampling rate
(6) The action of the cancellation (bucking) network

The following description of the AVTA system should be understood within the framework of these six points.

Figure A-1 is a partial block diagram of the AVTA system which

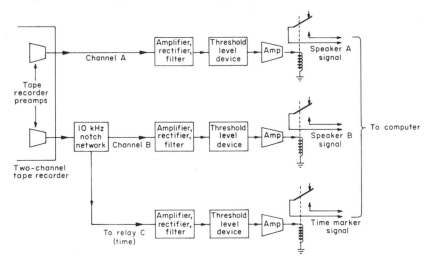

FIGURE A-1. A block diagram depicting the speaker and time interval channels of the AVTA system.

[2]We thank Prof. Louis J. Gerstman of City University of New York for focusing our attention on this aspect of Brady's work and clarifying its relevance to the understanding of our results.

is connected to the output of a two-channel tape recorder. The interview is so recorded that the voice of each participant is primarily confined to one channel. Each of the channels operates in the following manner. The audio signal of the associated speaker is amplified and rectified. The rectified signal is then filtered above 5 kHz producing a dc signal proportional to the intensity of the recorded voice. This signal is passed through a threshold level device. When the amplitude of the dc signal exceeds the preset threshold level, it actuates an amplifier-driven relay. The threshold level is set high enough to exclude random noise, but low enough to include the voice of the speaker when speaking softly. Thus, the state of the output relay (deenergized or energized) indicates the presence or absence of vocalization by the associated speaker. There are separate controls for the signal intensity, threshold, and time constant for each speaker's channel. The outputs of these relays are then sampled to generate the computer input. System operation requires an inquiry at regular intervals about the state of each of the relays. The inquiry command is initiated by an electronic timing device which may be set at any interval from 1 per second to 10 per second. At the selected rate, the computer receives the digitized dialogue pattern in the form of a two bit code.

In order to provide a time axis, a 10 kHz signal is superimposed upon one of the audiotape channels for a duration of 1 second at regular intervals during the initial recording. The AVTA system extracts the signal by passing it through the notch network shown in Figure A-1. The signal then actuates relay C as indicated in the drawing. Relay C is interconnected with a third input channel of the computer, and the time axis is used to automatically start and stop the processing for a preset number of minutes.[3]

The system thus far described would not adequately handle the problem created by the spilling of one speaker's voice into the microphone of the other. This unintended recording of one speaker's voice in the other's channel can cause both output relays to be actuated when only one participant is speaking. The relative prox-

---

[3]The state of each of the output relays is visually displayed by a lamp on the front panel. Thus, the lighting of a lamp signals an observer that its associated relay is energized. This visual display is the criterion for gain, threshold, and bucking adjustments so that the relay can be said to be tracking the on–off vocal pattern.

imity of each speaker's voice to his own microphone provides a considerable degree of attenuation of the voice of the nonintended speaker. The remainder of the nonintended vocal signal is cancelled electronically. The cancellation network shown in Figure A-2 carries an amount of signal from its intended channel sufficient

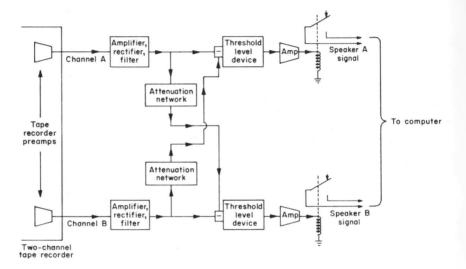

FIGURE A-2. A diagram of the placement of the nonintended signal cancellation network.

to subtract, or cancel, the effect of the recording of one speaker in the other speaker's channel. The amount of cancellation signal required depends upon such factors as the distance of the speakers from each other. The requirement for any particular recording is determined empirically by adjusting a control to the minimum setting required to eliminate the spilled signal. The use of this cancellation network permits flexibility in the experimental setting as well as the use of a wider range of microphones than could otherwise be employed.

Brady (1968) has shown that as thresholds are raised, vocalization lengths decrease and pause lengths increase, since long sounds of varying intensity may momentarily drop below the higher threshold and thus be broken into shorter ones, whereas a missed low level sound results in the splicing together of two pauses. This is also true of the AVTA system. Furthermore, our use of a time constant ("hangover") to smooth the envelope of the vocal signal by bridging pauses ≈ 200 milliseconds or less bears further discussion. The time constant (*TC*) of the AVTA system determines the time lag from the actual end of a vocalization to the point at which the relay opens. One may think of this in terms of a simple exponential decay function. The less the *TC*, the steeper the curve and the faster the cutoff. It is obviously affected by threshold level. Also within a given *TC*, the time to cutoff varies with the intensity of the voice since the exponential decay starts from a higher level. With the *TC* setting and average threshold used in our research, the loudest admissible signal has a *TC* of 300 milliseconds, the softest a *TC* of 0 milliseconds, and a voice of midrange intensity a *TC* of 150 milliseconds. The actual circuits differ from simple RC networks in two important respects. The rise time constant (i.e., the RC circuit through which a signal of *increasing* intensity is processed) is shorter than the decay time constant (i.e., the RC circuit through which a decaying or *decreasing* signal is processed). The rise time constant is set to be approximately one-sixth of the value of the decay time constant. The second respect in which it differs is that the decay network is not referenced to ground, but rather to a point slightly below ground. A decaying signal is not actually permitted to reach the reference level but is clamped at zero until the next positive signal arrives. This technique was employed in order to cut off the long tail of the exponential curve and utilize the more linear portion of the decay, thereby providing better control over the actual time to the point of cutoff. A negative bias was not used because this would also establish an additional threshold for an increasing signal.

Sampling rate is yet another variable to be reckoned with, since in our analog to digital conversion we assume that there was no sound between adjacent silence samples and no pause between adjacent vocalization samples. Were the rate too slow, we would run the risk of missing many short events, with resultant splicing together of their preceding and subsequent events. Schwartz (1968a, 1968b) analyzed the AVTA system from this viewpoint, and among the conclusions he reached are the following.

(1) A sampling rate greater than the mean on–off cycle is sufficient to prevent information loss. (Clearly the "naive" criterion of talking and pausing that we adopted in these analyses has an on–off cycle many times that of our 300 millisecond sampling interval.)

(2) In general, the larger the resolution factors, the larger the reported means.

(3) The observed average pause and average vocalization lengths are related to the true means through simultaneous equations dependent on the form of the distribution functions. A simulation with the assumption of exponential distributions indicates that the observed distributions remain exponential with means given by the simultaneous equations. Schwartz feels that this explains the relative agreement among various investigators regarding the shape of sound and silence distributions in spite of disparities in reported means.

In light of the foregoing argument, it is instructive to compare some of our means with those of Brady (1968); however, the methods are not quite comparable. Instead of sampling, as we do, at 300 millisecond intervals, he samples at 5 millisecond intervals. More importantly, he does not use a time constant to bridge pauses due to stop consonants, but rather he deletes all vocalizations ≤ 15 milliseconds and fills in all pauses ≤ 200 milliseconds. Some of his category definitions differ slightly from ours. We use his set of data for a threshold of -40 dBm. The percentages of silence, vocaliza-

TABLE A-1

SOME MEAN VALUES FROM FACE-TO-FACE DIALOGUES
REPORTED IN CHAPTER III AND COMPARABLE VALUES OBTAINED
BY BRADY (1968) IN 16 TELEPHONE CONVERSATIONS

Measure	Brady	Jaffe and Feldstein
Percent simultaneous speech	4.49	3.29
Percent joint silence	25.01	26.00
Percent vocalization (per speaker)	39.50	35.40
Mean vocalization	1.17 sec	1.64 sec
Mean pause	.50 sec	.66 sec
Mean switching pause	.40 sec	.77 sec
Mean simultaneous speech	.25 sec	.40 sec

tion, and simultaneous speech are remarkably alike since they are not affected by the differing sampling rates or the differing TCs. Our larger TC and resolution factor yield larger mean durations. The fact that his mean switching pause is shorter than his mean pause (contrary to our consistent findings of the opposite) may be referable to the telephone conversation. We lack comparable data, but the descriptive statistics for our second study of Chapter III (see Appendix D) indicate a tendency toward shorter switching pauses in those conversations which were held through an opaque screen.

To further complicate and conclude this discussion of what we mean by a speech detector, a discussion of our cancellation (bucking) circuit is in order since it may also affect the detection processes.

The bucking circuit cancels the unintended carryover of one speaker's voice in the other's channel. Maximum bucking is approximately 50% of the main channel signal. As the setting is increased for a speaker, the attenuation of *his* signal in the unintended channel is increased. For example, increasing the bucking for a speaker using channel 1 cancels the spill of his voice onto channel 2.

In processing the average recording, the bucking levels are kept nearly equal for both speakers. Most work thus far has called for the use of the upper-middle scale settings. Difficulty is occasionally encountered in cases where the record level is set too high for a given speaker. His voice will tend to saturate his own channel. When this occurs, the balance of the bucking network is upset, since an increase in his voice level will no longer result in an increased voltage in his own channel. However, since his voice level is lower in the nonintended channel, saturation will not as yet have taken place, thereby changing the ratio of nonintended channel signal level to intended channel signal level. An example may help to clarify this problem.

Assume that in a particular recording situation, a speaker's voice is recorded in the nonintended channel at one-fourth of the level that it is recorded in the intended channel. The bucking ratio required for attenuation, then, would be 1/4, or 25% (i.e., 25% of the intended channel signal would be necessary to cancel the nonintended signal). Assume further that 20 volts represent saturation level. Under these conditions, if a speaker's voice is loud enough to cause a 16 volt signal in his own channel, it would create a 4 volt signal in the nonintended channel, and a bucking setting of 25% would be adequate to cancel the unintended signal. If his voice now doubles in loudness, it would create a 32 volt signal in his own channel and an 8 volt signal in the nonintended channel. However, because of saturation, his own channel signal rises to only 20 volts. At a bucking setting of 25%, only 5 volts are available to cancel the 8 volt nonintended signal. This will not be sufficient, and his voice will be recorded in both channels as if simultaneous speech had taken place. Should such an error in recording occur, the best compromise solution would be to "overbuck." In this example, a 40% bucking level would accomplish the purpose. This *is* a compromise, however, since overbucking carries the disadvantage of cancelling some actual simultaneous speech. For example, should the aforementioned speaker talk at a 10 volt level, his bucking signal would be 4 volts (40%) even though his nonintended signal is only 2.5 volts (25%). This means that should the other speaker talk simultaneously below a 1.5 volt level, his voice signal would not be detected. The compromise is considered to be a fairly good solution because simultaneous speech is comparatively rare, and when it does occur it is not usually with such a large difference between the two speaker levels. The error it introduces, therefore, is relatively small.

APPENDIX B

RELIABILITY STUDIES OF THE AVTA SYSTEM

Two studies (unrelated to the studies reported in Chapter III) were conducted to evaluate the reliability of the AVTA system and to compare its performance to that of a highly trained operator. The first study was designed primarily to test the capacity of the component to detect low-level vocal signals reliably. For this purpose, the two participants were instructed to speak in relatively soft tones. The resulting 20 minute recording was a rather slowly paced conversation in which the incidence of simultaneous speech was comparatively rare. In the second study, the subjects were encouraged to speak freely in varying degrees of loudness. The first study did not produce sufficient simultaneous speech to permit generation of reliability figures in these categories. Therefore, in this second study, the subjects were instructed to interrupt each other frequently. In all other respects, no artificial structure was imposed. The recording was 30 minutes long, employing four speakers (two at a time).

The tape recordings were each analyzed on three different occasions, thereby generating three sets of data for each study. Product–moment correlation coefficients between paired occasions for all variables were computed. The reliability estimate for each variable is the average of the three correlation coefficients for that study. These data for the first and second reliability studies are presented in Tables B-1 and B-2, respectively. In the first, simultaneous speech occurred too infrequently to permit computation of reliability data in these categories.

A trained human operator was then required to perform the same function by pressing the appropriate switches as each subject spoke in the interview. (These switches were wired to replace the

TABLE B-1

RELIABILITY ESTIMATES OF THE AVTA SYSTEM AND A HUMAN OPERATOR
BASED UPON SUCCESSIVE 1 MINUTE SPEECH SAMPLES[a]

Variable	Component	Human operator
Total vocal time	.995	.895
Sum of switching pause durations	.916	.899
Sum of pause durations	.989	.873
Frequency distribution of pause durations	.997	.987

[a] Reliability Study I.

TABLE B-2

RELIABILITY ESTIMATES OF THE AVTA SYSTEM AND A HUMAN OPERATOR
BASED UPON SUCCESSIVE 2 MINUTE SPEECH SAMPLES[a]

Variable	Component	Human operator
Sum of simultaneous speech	.929	.634
Frequency of simultaneous speech	.918	.620
Frequency of utterances	.974	.721
Total vocal time	.999	.885
Sum of switching pause durations	.967	.679
Sum of pause durations	.988	.848
Frequency distribution of pause durations	.987	.939
Frequency distribution of simultaneous speech durations	.950	.888
Frequency distribution of switching pause durations	.977	.986

[a] Reliability Study II.

output relays of the AVTA system, thereby permitting the operator to simulate the system's function.) The averaged correlation coefficients of the three runs for the human operator were then computed as reliability estimates of human performance. These are also presented in Tables B-1 and B-2. For Study I, the data are based upon comparisons of successive 1 minute intervals for the summed time of the variables and for the frequency of the speech units. For Study II, the data are based upon successive 2 minute intervals. The histogram data reliability was computed by correlating the incidence of each variable for each successive interval on a total interview basis.

Examination of these data shows clearly that the reliability of the system is consistently higher than that of the trained operator. In addition, a comparison of the data from the two studies indicates that the trained operator's performance is seriously impaired when the recording contains a high incidence of simultaneous speech, whereas the reliability of the component is not noticeably affected by this condition. Saslow and Matarazzo (1959) also found, in a study utilizing the Interaction Chronograph, that interscorer reliability was lowest when the incidence of simultaneous speech increased. The advantages of automated electronic processing become apparent when task difficulty begins to tax the information processing abilities of human observers.

The reliability of the AVTA system is relatively independent of the quality of the tape recording. Errors introduced by sounds other than speech will not decrease the reliability of the system in that it will consistently record these. However, since the purpose of the system is to record the temporal patterns of speech, extraneous noise will decrease the validity of system operation. Thus, system validity is a function of the conditions of recording. While satisfactory recording conditions can be readily achieved, precautions must be taken to insure that such conditions are met. An operator, listening briefly to the recording while watching the output, can readily assess the extent to which irrelevant noise impairs the validity of the data.

USE OF THE NEYMAN-PEARSON STATISTIC FOR COMPARING MARKOV MODELS

We are interested in some measure of whether one model of a stochastic process fits the observed data better than another. One way of doing this is to compare the probability assigned to the data by the two models. *A priori*, the model which assigns the higher probabilities would appear to be preferable. In a large class of cases, the degree to which this assertion is justified may be precisely measured by the Neyman-Pearson Statistic (Billingsley, 1961), viz., minus two times the natural logarithm of the ratio of the two probabilities which may in these cases be shown to have, asymptotically, the distribution chi-square with an appropriate number of degrees of freedom.

Thus, for example, in many cases this statistic indicates the significance of the improvement achieved by increasing, in a predetermined manner, the number of parameters in the model. By "a predetermined manner" we will usually mean that the model with fewer parameters is a special case of that with the larger number of parameters. Imposition of additional restrictions on the more general case reduces it to the special case. This will be illustrated presently.

Let

f_{ij} = the frequency of a transition from state i at time t to state j at time $t+1$ in the more general case

L = the probability assigned to the data by the maximum likelihood transition probabilities p_{ij} under the assumptions of the more general case

$\hat{L}$ = the probability assigned to the data by the maximum likelihood transition probabilities $\hat{p}_{ij}$ under the assumptions of the special case.

Then

$$L = \prod_{ij} p_{ij}{}^{f_{ij}} \tag{1}$$

and

$$\hat{L} = \prod_{ij} \hat{p}_{ij}{}^{f_{ij}} \tag{2}$$

The Neyman-Pearson Statistic (NPS) is then

$$- 2 \log_e \frac{\hat{L}}{L} \tag{3}$$

Substituting (1) and (2) in (3), we get

$$\text{NPS} = - 2 \sum_{ij} f_{ij} \log_e \frac{\hat{p}_{ij}}{p_{ij}}$$

The general case always assigns the highest probability to the observed data, so $L \geqslant \hat{L}$. If $L = \hat{L}$, then NPS = 0, and the larger numbers of parameters contribute no extra information. We may then say that the additional restrictions of the special case result in a model which fits the data as well as the general case. The extra parameters are redundant. If $L > \hat{L}$, the significance of the NPS value is given by a chi-square table with the appropriate number of degrees of freedom. The problem of interpreting the significance levels in light of a large number of samples is discussed in Chapter IV.

This statistic was used in Chapter IV for the following comparisons:

(a) Comparison of the four-state single-source model (12 parameters) with the normative model (12 parameters). Although each has the same number of parameters, the latter is the special case in that it was the average transition matrix for a randomly selected group of conversations and could not be expected to fit any particular dialogue perfectly unless that dialogue were representative of the mean of its population.

(b) Comparison of the four-state single-source model (12 parameters) with the four-state independent decision model (8 parameters). The special restriction on the latter was that $\hat{p}_{i1}\hat{p}_{i2} = \hat{p}_{i0}\hat{p}_{i3}$, $(i = 0,1,2,3)$.

(c) Comparison of two separate four-state single-source models (correctly matched and randomly mismatched) with each of two four-state independent decision models (expected and predicted). This was the predictive experiment reported in Section III.

In Chapter V, the NPS was used for:

(d) Comparison of the six-state single-source model (18 parameters) with the four-state single-source model (12 parameters). The latter is the special case under the restrictions of the lumpability hypothesis for the separate silence and simultaneous speech states. The restrictions are stated in Equations (2) and (3) of Chapter V.

Thus, the four-state single-source model can be compared with both the four-state normative and four-state independent decision models as in (a) and (b), since each is a special case of it. Similarly, in (c) the correctly and randomly mismatched matrices represent competitive general cases. These three-way comparisons allow a choice between competing models when, as in our case, the number of observations is so large that NPS is almost always significant.

APPENDIX D

DESCRIPTIVE STATISTICS FOR THE THREE EXPERIMENTS DESCRIBED IN CHAPTER III

TABLE D-1

MEANS (M) AND STANDARD DEVIATIONS (SD) OF THE SUBJECTS' AVERAGE DURATIONS (IN SECONDS) OF PAUSES (P), SWITCHING PAUSES (SP), AND VOCALIZATIONS (V) FOR THE FOUR INTERVIEWS OF THE FIRST EXPERIMENT[a]

Parameter		Interview			
		I	II	III	IV
P	M	.934	.837	.766	.934
	SD	.372	.339	.330	.337
SP	M	1.555	1.243	1.442	1.161
	SD	.380	.399	.375	.393
V	M	1.683	2.058	1.901	1.955
	SD	.316	.314	.317	.316

[a] The N for each mean is 50. The table entries are based upon proportionality constants which were converted to average durations with the formula, $M = 1/(1 - PC)$. Each interview lasted 16 minutes.

TABLE D-2

Means (M) and Standard Deviations (SD) of the Average Durations (in Seconds) of Pauses for Subject Sex, Conditions (V, S), Order (VS, SV), and Occasions (O) of the Second Experiment[a]

			Condition			
			V		S	
			M	SD	M	SD
O_1	Male	VS	.670	.144	.669	.138
		SV	.645	.160	.650	.146
	Female	VS	.616	.115	.728	.323
		SV	.632	.100	.567	.096
O_2	Male	VS	.767	.276	.668	.151
		SV	.650	.223	.655	.256
	Female	VS	.628	.127	.611	.169
		SV	.670	.260	.608	.229
O_3	Male	VS	.652	.117	.656	.130
		SV	.640	.164	.632	.129
	Female	VS	.767	.303	.783	.293
		SV	.617	.276	.581	.262

[a] V stands for the vis-à-vis condition, S for the "screen" condition. The order sequences VS and SV indicate which condition occurred first. Each mean is based upon the average durations of eight subjects. The dialogue of each condition lasted 20 minutes.

TABLE D-3

MEANS AND STANDARD DEVIATIONS OF THE AVERAGE DURATIONS
(IN SECONDS) OF SWITCHING PAUSES FOR SUBJECT SEX, CONDITIONS (V, S),
ORDER (VS, SV), AND OCCASIONS (O) OF THE SECOND EXPERIMENT[a]

			Condition			
			V		S	
			M	SD	M	SD
O_1	Male	VS	.869	.268	.774	.252
		SV	.773	.200	.781	.261
	Female	VS	1.000	.430	1.060	.515
		SV	.881	.282	.865	.461
O_2	Male	VS	.820	.200	.787	.245
		SV	.815	.348	.745	.269
	Female	VS	.927	.358	.815	.273
		SV	.850	.321	.809	.330
O_3	Male	VS	.786	.195	.782	.302
		SV	.784	.216	.848	.222
	Female	VS	1.341	1.116	1.257	.826
		SV	.987	.720	.780	.378

[a] See the note of Table D-2.

TABLE D-4

Means and Standard Deviations of the Average Durations
(in Seconds) of Vocalizations for Subject Sex, Conditions (V, S),
Order (VS, SV), and Occasions (O) of the Second Experiment[a]

			Condition			
			V		S	
			M	SD	M	SD
O_1	Male	VS	1.635	.325	1.570	.226
		SV	1.662	.317	1.751	.394
	Female	VS	1.707	.396	1.688	.258
		SV	1.532	.347	1.688	.372
O_2	Male	VS	1.621	.398	1.602	.227
		SV	1.733	.646	1.817	.675
	Female	VS	1.619	.303	1.624	.349
		SV	1.711	.789	1.741	.588
O_3	Male	VS	1.545	.237	1.694	.298
		SV	1.736	.421	1.727	.379
	Female	VS	1.651	.436	1.684	.402
		SV	1.624	.768	1.600	.684

[a] See note of Table D-2.

TABLE D-5

MEANS AND STANDARD DEVIATIONS OF THE AVERAGE DURATIONS
(IN SECONDS) OF SIMULTANEOUS SPEECH FOR DYAD SEX (MM, FF, MF),
CONDITIONS (V, S), ORDER (VS, SV), AND OCCASIONS (O) OF THE
SECOND EXPERIMENT[a]

| | | | Condition | | | |
| | | | V | | S | |
			M	SD	M	SD
O_1	MM	VS	.379	.333	.399	.329
		SV	.413	.327	.405	.328
	FF	VS	.447	.338	.438	.349
		SV	.413	.312	.412	.334
O_2	MF	VS	.414	.334	.404	.333
		SV	.437	.331	.415	.331
O_3	MM	VS	.415	.324	.392	.332
		SV	.449	.320	.411	.326
	FF·	VS	.438	.334	.404	.328
		SV	.427	.330	.385	.319

[a]V stands for the vis-à-vis condition, S for the "screen" condition. The order sequences VS and SV indicate which condition occurred first. Each mean of O_1 and O_3
is based upon eight observations; each mean of O_2 is based upon 16 observations.
MM indicates that the dyad consisted of two males, FF, that it consisted of two
females, and MF that it consisted of a male and female.

TABLE D-6

MEANS AND STANDARD DEVIATIONS OF THE AVERAGE DURATIONS
(IN SECONDS) OF PAUSES (P), SWITCHING PAUSES (SP), VOCALIZATIONS (V),
SIMULTANEOUS SPEECH (SS), AND THE FREQUENCY OF SPEAKER SWITCHES
(SSW) FOR THE EIGHT OCCASIONS OF THE THIRD EXPERIMENT[a]

Parameter		Occasions								Average
		1	2	3	4	5	6	7	8	
P	M	.593	.593	.590	.597	.593	.590	.602	.611	.596
	SD	.087	.091	.083	.090	.089	.098	.097	.111	.093
SP	M	.662	.653	.654	.664	.662	.641	.680	.695	.664
	SD	.144	.145	.140	.169	.174	.166	.194	.187	.165
V	M	1.300	1.352	1.389	1.435	1.410	1.501	1.505	1.472	1.420
	SD	.372	.331	.350	.377	.367	.350	.467	.398	.376
SS	M	.399	.412	.401	.442	.414.	.413	.416	.411	.413
	SD	.033	.034	.030	.195	.036	.028	.039	.048	.055
SSW	M	188.9	193.3	187.8	185.5	192.9	191.2	191.6	198.8	191.3
	SD	41.3	32.6	39.3	38.2	44.7	40.3	41.8	45.9	40.5

[a] Each mean is based upon 72 observations since each of the 24 subjects has three values derived from her interaction with three other subjects. Each dialogue lasted 30 minutes.

REFERENCES

Anderson, S. W., & Jaffe, J. *Projections between memory codes and some speech events not derivable from stimulus–response theory.* Scientific Report No. 5. New York: Dept. of Communication Sciences, New York State Psychiatric Institute, 1970.

Anderson, T. W., & Goodman, L. A. Statistical inference about Markov chains. *Annals of Mathematical Statistics,* 1957, **28,** 89–110.

Baumrin, J. A. Absolute judgments of the duration of a silent interval. *Proceedings of the 77th Annual Convention of the American Psychological Association,* 1969, **4,** 13–14.

Billingsley, P. *Statistical inference for Markov processes.* Chicago: University of Chicago Press, 1961.

Boomer, D. S. Hesitation and grammatical coding. *Language and Speech,* 1965, **8,** 148–158.

Brady, P. T. A statistical analysis of on-off patterns in 16 conversations. *Bell System Technical Journal,* 1968, **47,** 73–91.

Brady, P. T. A model for generating on-off speech patterns in two-way conversation. Paper presented at the annual meeting of the Acoustical Society of America, Philadelphia, April 1969.

Cassotta, L., Feldstein, S., & Jaffe, J. AVTA: A device for automatic vocal transaction analysis. *Journal of the Experimental Analysis of Behavior,* 1964, **7,** 99–104.

Cassotta, L., Feldstein, S., & Jaffe, J. *The stability and modifiability of individual vocal characteristics in stress and nonstress interviews.* Research Bulletin No. 2. New York: William Alanson White Institute, 1967.

Cassotta, L., Jaffe, J., Feldstein, S., & Moses, R. *Operating manual: Automatic Vocal Transaction Analyzer.* Research Bulletin No. 1. New York: William Alanson White Institute, 1964.

Chapple, E. D. Quantitative analysis of the interaction of individuals. *Proceedings of the National Academy of Sciences, U.S.,* 1939, **25,** 58–67.

Chapple, E. D. The Interaction Chronograph: Its evolution and present application. *Personnel,* 1949, **25,** 295–307.

Cherry, C. *On human communication: A review, a survey, and a criticism.* New York: Science Editions, 1961.

Collins, M. E. Dissimulation factors in attitude measurements: A factor analytic study of White Americans toward the American Negro. Paper presented at the Social Psychology Seminar, Columbia University, April 1964.

Cooper, F. S. Describing the speech process in motor command terms. *Journal of the*

143

Acoustical Society of America, 1966, **39**, 1221. (Abstract) (Status Report of Speech Research, Haskins Laboratories, 1966, SR–5/6, 2.1–2.27.)

Dittman, A. T., & Llewellyn, L. G. The phonemic clause as a unit of speech decoding. *Journal of Personality and Social Psychology,* 1967, **6**, 341–349.

Dittman, A. T., & Llewellyn, L. G. Body movement and speech rhythm in social conversation. *Journal of Personality and Social Psychology,* 1969, **11**, 98–106.

Edwards, W. Tactical note on the relation between scientific and statistical hypotheses. *Psychological Bulletin,* 1965, **63**, 400–402.

Feldstein, S. Interspeaker influence in conversational interaction. *Psychological Reports,* 1968, **22**, 826–828.

Feldstein, S., Jaffe, J., & Cassotta, L. Mathematically predicted time patterns of dialogue. Paper presented at the meeting of the Eastern Psychological Association, New York, April 1966.

Feldstein, S., Jaffe, J., & Cassotta, L. The effect of mutual visual access upon conversational time patterns. *American Psychologist,* 1967, **23**, 594. (Abstract)

Fries, C. C. *The structure of English.* New York: Harcourt, Brace & World, 1952.

Gerstman, L. J., Feldstein, S., & Jaffe, J. Syntactical versus temporal cues for speaker switching in natural dialogue. Paper presented at the meeting of the Acoustical Society of America, Miami, Florida, November 1967.

Goldman-Eisler, F. Speech analysis and mental process. *Language and Speech,* 1958, **1**, 59–75.

Goldman-Eisler, F. *Psycholinguistics.* New York: Academic Press, 1968.

Haggard, E. A. *Intraclass correlation and the analysis of variance.* New York: Dryden, 1958.

Hargreaves, W. A. A model for speech unit duration. *Language and Speech,* 1960, **3**, 164–173.

Hargreaves, W. A., & Starkweather, J. A. Collection of temporal data with the Duration Tabulator. *Journal of the Experimental Analysis of Behavior,* 1959, **2**, 179–183.

Jakobson, R. Discussant of "Factors and forms of aphasia" by A. R. Luria. In A. V. S. de Reuck & M. O'Connor (Eds.), *Ciba Foundation Symposium on disorders of language.* Boston: Little, Brown, 1964. Pp. 162–182.

Jaffe, J. *Linked probablistic finite automata: A model for the temporal interaction of speakers.* Scientific Report No. 1. New York: Dept. of Communication Sciences, New York State Psychiatric Institute, 1967.

Jaffe, J. Computer assessment of dyadic interaction rules from chronographic data. In J. Shlein (Ed.), *Research in psychotherapy.* Vol. 3. Washington, D.C.: American Psychological Association, 1968.

Jaffe, J., & Norman, D. A simulation of the time patterns of dialogue. Scientific Report No. CS–4. Center for Cognitive Studies, Harvard University, 1964.

Jaffe, J., Cassotta, L., & Feldstein, S. Markovian model of time patterns of speech. *Science,* 1964, **144**, 884–886.

Jaffe, J., Feldstein, S., & Cassotta, L. A stochastic model of speaker switching in natural dialogue. In K. Salzinger & S. Salzinger (Eds.), *Research in verbal behavior and some neurophysiological implications.* New York: Academic Press, 1967. (a)

Jaffe, J., Feldstein, S., & Cassotta, L. Markovian models of dialogic time patterns.

Nature, 1967, **216**, 93–94. (b)

Jaffe, J., Breskin, S., & Gerstman, L. J. On the range of sequential constraint in monolog rythyms. *Psychonomic Science*, 1970. (In press.)

Kasl, S., & Mahl, G. A simple device for obtaining certain verbal activity measures during interviews. *Journal of Abnormal and Social Psychology*, 1956, **53**, 388–390.

Kemeny, J. C., & Snell, J. L. *Finite Markov Chains*. Princeton, New Jersey: D. Van Nostrand, 1960.

Liberman, A. M., Harris, K. S., Eimas, P., Lisker, L., & Bastian, J. An effect of learning on speech perception: The discrimination of durations of silence with and without phonemic significance. *Language and Speech*, 1961, **4**, 175–195.

Liberman, A. M., Cooper, F. S., Shankweiler, D. P., & Studdert-Kennedy, M. Perception of the speech code. *Psychological Review*, 1967, **74**, 431–461.

Mahl, G. F. Measuring the patient's anxiety during interviews from "expressive" aspects of his speech. *Transactions of the New York Academy of Sciences*, 1959, **21**, 249–257.

Matarazzo, J. D., Wiens, A. N., Saslow, G., Allen, B. V., & Weitman, M. Interviewer mm-hmm and interviewee speech durations. *Psychotherapy: Theory, Research & Practice*, 1964, **1**, 109–114.

Meltzer, L., Hayes, D. P., & Shellenberger, D. Consistency of vocal behavior in discussions. Paper presented at the meeting of the American Psychological Association, Chicago, September 1966.

Miller, G. A. Speaking in general. Review of J. H. Greenberg (Ed.), *Universals of language. Contemporary Psychology*, 1963, **8**, 417–418.

Miller, G. A., Galanter, E., & Pribram, K. H. *Plans and the structure of behavior.* New York: Holt, Rinehart & Winston, 1964.

Mosteller, F. Memorandum C: A model for speech and silence distributions. Unpublished manuscript on the Verzeano-Finesinger Analyzer, Harvard University, 1949.

Norwine, A. C., & Murphy, O. J. Characteristic time intervals in telephonic conversation. *Bell System Technical Journal*, 1938, **17**, 281–291.

Ray, M. L., & Webb, E. J. Speech duration effects in the Kennedy news conferences. *Science*, 1966, **153**, 899–901.

Saslow, G., & Matarazzo, J. D. A technique for studying changes in interview behavior. In E. A. Rubenstein & M. B. Parloff (Eds.), *Research in psychotherapy.* Washington, D. C.: American Psychological Association, 1959.

Schwartz, J. *Analog–digital conversion at slow sampling rates. Application to the automatic vocal transaction analyzer.* Scientific Report No. 2, Part A. New York: Dept. of Communication Sciences, New York State Psychiatric Institute, 1968. (a).

Schwartz, J. *Effect of finite resolution in the measurement of interarrival and discharge times.* Scientific Report No. 2, Part B. New York: Dept. of Communication Sciences, New York State Psychiatric Institute, 1968. (b).

Schwartz, J., & Jaffe, J. Markovian prediction of sequential temporal patterns in spontaneous speech. *Language and Speech*, 1968, **11**, 27–30.

Shapiro, D. Group learning of speech sequences without awareness. *Science*, 1964, **144**, 74–75.

Shapiro, D. Group learning of speech sequences without awareness. *Science,* 1964, **144,** 74–75.

Siegman, A. W., & Pope, B. Effects of question specificity and anxiety-producing messages on verbal fluency in the initial interview. *Journal of Personality and Social Psychology,* 1965, **2,** 522–530.

Sullivan, H. S. *Conceptions of modern psychiatry.* New York: Norton, 1947.

Trager, G. L., & Smith, H. L., Jr. *An outline of English structure. (Studies in linguistics: Occasional papers.* No. 3.) Norman, Okla.: Battenberg Press, 1951. (Republished: New York, American Council of Learned Societies, 1965.)

Verzeano, M., & Finesinger, J. An automatic analyzer for the study of speech in interaction and in free association. *Science,* 1949, **110,** 45–46.

Welkowitz, J., & Feldstein, S. Dyadic interaction and induced differences in perceived similarity. *Proceedings of the 77th Annual Convention of the American Psychological Association,* 1969, **4,** 343–344.

Wiens, A. N., Molde, D., Holman, D., & Matarazzo, J. D. Can interview interaction measures be taken from tape recordings? *Journal of Psychology,* 1966, **63,** 249–260.

Wiens, A. N., Saslow, G., Matarazzo, J. D., & Allen, B. Interruption behavior during interviews: A detailed analysis. Paper presented at the annual meeting of the Western Psychological Association, Santa Monica, California, April 1963.

Subject Index

A

Absorption probabilities, 102

Acoustic phonetics, 2

Action, interaction chronography and, 13, 15

Age, experimental design and, 29

Ambiguity, 41

Analog to digital conversion, 51
dyadic states and, 118
linguistic information and, 21–22
punched paper tape and, 17–18, 20, 21
sampling rate and, *see* Sampling rate
vocal signal and, *see* Vocal signal

Analog to digital converter, *see* Automatic Vocal Transaction Analyzer, (AVTA)

Anthropology, 6
language development and, 113
social, 1

Anxiety, speech disruption and, 40

Articulation, 6

Asynchrony, 11

Attention, 114
speaker switch and, 10

Automatic Vocal Transaction Analyzer (AVTA), 51, 115
compared to human operator, 131–133
computer and, 17, 123
description of, 17–18, 20, 123–130
interaction chronography and, 123
sampling rate and, *see* Sampling rate
simulation and, 132
speech detector and, *see* Speech detector
voice relay and, *see* Voice relay

"Awkward silence," Markov model and, 79

B

Background noise, 124

Behavior,
conventional language, 6
noninferential classification of, 14–16
quantification of, 1

Behavioral state, *see* State

Boundary,
pause and, 28, 77–78, 79, 111
symmetrical events and, 78
time domain and, *see* Time domain

Boundary markings, speaker switching and, 49–50

Breathing, 5, 63

C

Cancellation network, 124, 126, 129–130

Channel, 17, 50
cancellation network and, *see* Cancellation network
"one-way," 11
operation of, 125

Cheering, 11

Chi-square test, 74, 84

Classification, *see* Descriptive classification

Coding, *see* Decoding; Encoding

Communication,
disordered, rules of dialogue and, 6
telegraphic or radio, "one-way channel" model and, 11

147